Hearing Men's Voices

Also by Roy McCloughry

Aids: A Christian Response
(with Carol Bebawi)
Ethical Tensions in the Welfare State
Debt
(with Andrew Hartropp)
Taking Action
The Eye of the Needle
Men and Masculinity: From Power to Love
Men without Masks
(with Roger Murphy)
Population Growth and Christian Ethics
Belief in Politics: People, Policies and Personal Faith

Hearing Men's Voices

Men in Search of Their Soul

Roy McCloughry

Hodder & Stoughton
LONDON SYDNEY AUCKLAND

British Library Cataloguing in Publication Data
A record for this book is available from the British Library

ISBN 0 340 63038 8

Typeset by Avon Dataset Ltd, Bidford-on-Avon, Warks

Printed and bound in Great Britain by
The Guernsey Press Co. Ltd, Channel Isles

Hodder & Stoughton Ltd
A Division of Hodder Headline PLC
338 Euston Road
London NW1 3BH

For

Steve Barber
Rod Beadles
David Elliman
Glynn Harrison
Martyn Offord
Steve Stickley

Contents

Acknowledgements

I am grateful to both the interviewers on this project who were Ms Heidi Shewell-Cooper (interviews 1–12), and Dr Kaja Ziesler (13–38). Their expertise as interviewers and their insights and analyses contributed in large part to the success of the project. Kaja Ziesler deserves a special thanks for transcribing all the interviews and writing reports on the project which were a model of clarity. I am indebted to Prof. Roger Murphy of the University of Nottingham for his commitment to this project and for his role in managing the conduct of the research interviews, which were carried out under the joint auspices of the School of Education and Kingdom Trust. I would also like to thank the Kirby Laing Trust for the grant which made this work possible.

Others contributed in various ways and I would like to thank the members of the men's group of which I have been a member for the last ten years. The book is dedicated to them. I would like to thank Emma Torrance, Sarah Holt, Charlotte Meldrum and Michèle Taylor, as well as Andy and Julia Ogden for all they contributed to this book. My editors at Hodder and Stoughton, Annabel Robson and David Moloney have been supportive throughout. Lastly, my thanks, as ever, go to Helen, Joanna, Lizzie and Lauren, the only women's group of which I will ever be a member, for putting up with my not noticing that anyone in the room was talking to me while this book was in its final stages.

Preface

This book is both unique and remarkable due to the willingness of dozens of men to talk about the stories of their lives. In a society which stereotypes men as irresponsible, mute and un-caring, here are men who blow stereotypes apart to reveal a sex grappling with the demands of a new kind of society. They believe that they have little to offer in talking about spirituality, masculinity or their emotional life. But, having said that, they then talk in a way which is compelling about the celebrations and tragedies of their lives. Perhaps what is most surprising is the lack of self-confidence so many of them admit to.

Hearing Men's Voices was conceived after the very positive response to *Men and Masculinity: From Power to Love* (London: Hodder, 1992). I became interested in the extent to which that book's analysis of masculinity and spirituality was owned by other men. Since then I have talked to hundreds of men, both personally, and in retreats, conferences and local churches, who have confirmed that these issues are important for them even though they are rarely discussed.

I became interested in the growth and development of men's groups and co-authored a book with Prof. Roger Murphy, of the School of Education at the University of Nottingham, entitled *Men without Masks* (Cambridge: Grove, 1994) and based on research carried out under the joint auspices of the School of Education and Kingdom Trust.

This third project arose from my conviction that the crisis in masculinity we were hearing so much about was related to the spiritual confusion which is evident at the end of the twentieth century.

I wanted to root this exploration in the stories of men, hence the interviews drawn on here with thirty-eight men from Nottinghamshire. The interviews ran to hundreds of thousands of words and I have only been able to give a brief impression of the kind of responses these men gave to the issues raised. The men were found either through advertising, or introduction through third parties, and they first filled out a short form outlining their approach to the project's aims, which were explained to them. They were asked if they could give an hour of their time and were informed that the interview would be recorded and transcribed. They were assured that only those directly involved in the project would see the transcription and their anonymity would be guaranteed. In the book, details which could be used to identify them, including names, have been changed.

The men were interviewed by one of two researchers, both women. The questions were open-ended and designed to enable the interviewees to talk about their lives rather than feel they were answering a question. Some of the questions changed over the course of the interviews, mostly to help interviewees respond with more ease. For example, asking open-ended questions about spirituality became (for the last few interviews) responses to flash cards with the words prayer, worship and spirituality on them.

There is nothing special about the number thirty-eight. We were not trying to take a sample of representative men through-out the country nor even in Nottinghamshire. Such a project would have been beyond our scope. The essence of our project was to show what a few dozen men would say about their lives, beliefs, relationships and work. We believed that even thirty-eight men would provide a rich resource of material with which men everywhere would resonate. This has turned out to be the case in a very remarkable way.

All interviews have strengths and weaknesses, and several things have to be considered in interpreting them. The interviewees may have tailored their answers to the theme of the project, or given answers which they thought we wanted. In reading the interviews we did not feel that this was the case except on one or two occasions, but the reader ought to bear this in mind.

The quotations in this book have been edited where conversational style was in conflict with a clear reading of the text, where an interviewee wandered off the point he was making but returned to it later, was repetitive or where details needed to be taken out to preserve anonymity.

It would be the height of irony if, in writing a book whose purpose is to let the reader hear men's voices, I then imposed my own agenda on it. It is difficult to let people speak directly to the reader without wanting to tidy up or defend a position which they are attacking but this is what I have set out to do and hope I have achieved. My own voice is, of course, heard throughout the book, reflecting on the issues raised. But, whilst in some books one is led to a conclusion by the author, it is up to the reader to make up his or her own mind about the content of this one.

One thing stood out about the interviewees. They were generous not only in opening up their homes to us but also in being willing to talk so openly about their lives, especially when doing so was difficult and painful at times. I am grateful to them. Without them this book would not have been possible.

Lastly, I should say something about my own perspective. I am a Christian and so for me spirituality simply means living out the Christian life, which is based on the life, death and resurrection of Jesus Christ. I accept the belief of the Church that Jesus is 'fully God and fully man' and that the Holy Spirit is given to us to enable us to become like Christ. For me, life is a pilgrimage from Christian belief to Christlike character, a journey which is always incomplete and which is only possible because of the generosity of God's forgiveness and love. I understand the frustrations many of the men interviewed here have about Christianity and the Church, and share some of them, but the fact remains that I am still committed to both, seeing in the one the source of hope for the world and, in the other, the hesitant beginnings of a new way of being community.

My own calling is to work on the interface between the Church and the world outside it, trying to make some sense of the social, economic and political issues we are facing but doing so in a way which is distinctively Christian. Readers may wonder why, if this is so, there is so little formal theology in this book. Partly it is because I am a social scientist and not a professional theologian. It is also because my other book on this subject fulfilled that purpose. In many senses this book comes before it and leads into it. But I also like to think that in this book it is the method which matters. Listening conveys love, and if ever a society needed to rediscover that, it is ours.

I

What is Man?

It is easy to get distracted from thinking about how our lives are going. We do not live in a society which encourages us to reflect, nor do we find it easy to get the space and the quiet to do it. Being busy is a very modern way of showing others that our days are full, even if our hearts are empty. Presumably a businessman is a man who is paid for being busy. But as those who are not in employment know, pace is not the same as purpose. Depending on being busy or having momentum is a distraction from asking, 'How am I doing?'.

Ignoring our deepest needs becomes routine when we lose the language to express who we are. We are simply not sure anymore. We can talk of where we were born, who our parents are and describe our personal history, but we are not aware that there is something missing. We have lost the ability to put our lives in the context of a Big Story, by which we make sense of life. The Big Story tells us about the creation of the world and of our beginnings. It tells of the distortion and frustration of the world, God's intervention to save it and the possibility of a new world coming. Our personal history makes sense when placed in the context of the Big Story. But our sunday supplement society never mentions it. As far as the media is concerned, it never existed.

So we now live in the visible world of *things*. We make them, consume them, replace them, desire them, save for them, discuss them . . . our lives revolve around them. We do not see that an invisible world has any relevance to the unseen struggles in our lives or that what we desire dominates our lives. There is a big divide between those who desire to consume the world's goods and those who are consumed by their desire for God. It was the Big Story which gave our own lives purpose and meaning and its loss has had a devastating impact on us.

People often talk of the soul as something we possess as if it were the spiritual equivalent of an invisible liver or kidney. But a soul is not something we possess, it is a description of the person we are. It is the opposite to seeing ourselves as a chance collection of atoms. Seeing ourselves as soul means that we accept that our lives have meaning and purpose from our birth. The reason is that the word 'soul', or 'spirit', which is the same word, means 'the breath of God'. We are not only living souls rather than machines or animals but we are 'made in God's image' which means that in some way God has made us like himself.

In our culture we are beginning to miss that dimension of our lives. We are the first culture in the history of the world to claim that there is nothing beyond ourselves, to which we are accountable. So it is possible, and may be now almost routine, for us to live as though that image were not there and ignore our spirituality. If so, then we can wither like grapes on a vine which are starved of light. We may make the mistake of thinking that spirituality is for religious people rather than something which covers every area of life. After all, if God is there his world contains everything from the Psalms to the *Archers*, to the offside rule. Restrict God to what goes on in churches for an hour or so on Sundays and you have reduced spirituality down to such insignificance that it can be ignored. Look up at the stars on a cold clear night in winter and see it as divine handiwork and suddenly God seems very big and we feel very small.

So the context in which we see ourselves matters. There are four main areas to look at. The men interviewed here, many of whom are not religious, some of whom were religious, and some who are religious, speak about their own views on spirituality in relation to God, relationships with others, work and their own identity. These are the areas through which human beings have expressed themselves and by which they have been identified since the opening chapters of the Bible.

First then we turn to male identity. In what follows I talk of masculinity and use that word to refer to the expectations, myths and interpretations by which men see their lives. The word 'male' I use more for the biology and genetic inheritance of men. Of course, in reality they cannot be separated but this book is more about masculinity than it is about maleness. How *do* men see themselves?

The Impact of Changing Roles

You don't have to go back as far as Jane Austen to find men and women living in different worlds. Only a generation ago men and women were seen as different from one another. It was this difference which was the foundation of marriage and the home. Men operated in the public realm and women in the private. Men were the providers for the family and women the home-makers and carers of children and extended family. There was little freedom to challenge these roles and those who did were seen as subversive. The virtue of this way of doing things was that everybody knew what was required of them. However, there was little freedom to exhibit characteristics which were only meant to belong to the other gender. To be 'different' meant to be under strain, 'sex-role strain'.

There are many people in contemporary society that still prefer to live in this way. But for most of us things have changed out of all recognition. Men and women no longer live in hermetically sealed and separate worlds. Opportunities exist for men and women to have more choice in the way they live their lives. Our emphasis is not on the strict rules which kept men and women apart but on the intimacy men and women enjoy.

There is a truce in the sex war. We borrow emotions, careers and characteristics from one another which were previously denied us. This relatively new way of operating has its strengths but it also has weaknesses. There is increasing freedom of choice but with it has come a loss of definition and a confusion about what is expected of men and women. It seems that there are costs to us whether society is organised according to social hierarchy or personal freedom.

At the moment women are able to take advantage of a wider range of choices to demonstrate that they are not only as capable as men but in some cases more capable. Instead of being constrained by the roles to which society tied them they are now able to express their individuality and their gifting. It is amazing how quickly men seem to have lost their confidence and collude about extending low opinions about men in general. As Patrick said,

I think my older daughter thinks men are a waste of space and I wholeheartedly agree, on the whole.

The Challenge of Identity

So, much as we welcome a truce in the sex war, there is a downside. The uncertainties which have arisen from these changes are being felt by both men and women. If the roles and duties which previously defined male identity can be so effectively challenged that nothing can ever be the same again, what is left? Where there was once a sacred foundation there is now a question mark. Not only is there confusion but there is an undercurrent of accusation. Men are not only in the fog, they are in the dock.

Sam Keen, a well-known American writer on masculinity and spirituality, puts these dilemmas well when he says,

Ask almost any man, 'how does it feel to be a man these days? Do you feel manhood is honoured, respected, celebrated?' Those who pause long enough to consider their gut feeling will likely tell you they feel blamed, demeaned and attacked. But their reactions may be pretty vague. Many men feel that they are involved in a night battle against a foe. Voices from the surrounding darkness shout hostile challenges: 'Men are too aggressive. Too soft. Too insensitive. Too macho. Too power-mad. Too much like little boys. Too wimpy. Too violent. Too obsessed with sex. Too detached to care. Too busy. Too rational. Too lost to lead. Too dead to feel.' Exactly what we are supposed to become is not clear.[1]

In the past men's lives were bound up with work, institutions and roles and it is easy to see how they adjusted to the expectations and demands of those roles. Now things are changing. We are moving from being an institutional society to a relational society. This poses a key dilemma for men. Can they move from competition to connection? The strength of such a society is founded on the community and the relationships within it. Can men form close friendships with others, particularly with other men? As we shall see, men need friends other than their wives and partners. Longevity adds to our need for relationship. We are all living longer and retirement will be very empty if we have not learned how to form relationships with other people.

In a relational society it is no longer possible to assume that people are defined by roles or by occupation. The only way of understanding a person is by listening. As men emerge from their roles blinking in the light of day they find a new emphasis on their individuality. They are no longer as protected by their employment or their social role because these are now shared by women. So they are not only looking for a new gender identity – what is a man? – but a new personal identity – who am I? Such is the agenda facing modern men. Only by listening to men can we find out what the world looks like from their perspective.

The Challenge of Expression

A society characterised by hierarchy and power brought tragic consequences for both men and women. First, women had their achievements suppressed; second, men had their feelings suppressed. The first is the challenge of *oppression*. The second is the challenge of *expression*. As society has changed women have effectively challenged oppression and society is changing as a result. One of the reasons it has changed is that women combined with one another to express a corporate solidarity. Women were not alone, they were together. Their strength was in building a campaign against injustice on the foundations of women's collective empathy with one another. Their aim was to change the society and the effectiveness of their campaigns could be measured by changes in the law, increased access to institutions and social change. By supporting one another women's consciousness also changed.

The task facing men is different. It is difficult to know how many men welcome the changes feminism brought with it but young men do not know any other world. Equality, opportunity and anti-discrimination policy are all positive changes for both men and women. But where women have gained something, there is an uneasy feeling among men that they have lost something. This does not mean that the new opportunities for women should be reversed or even resented. The overthrow of fixed roles meant freedom for women but it also meant a loss of identity for those men who had become over-identified with them. If men prided themselves in having the strength and bravery to be firemen (for instance), then when women became firewomen this was no longer a masculine preserve. In terms of equality men may welcome this, although many will find it difficult. But in women joining previous all-male occupations the question is raised, what is distinctive about being a man? After all men used to identify themselves with particular work roles because it was thought that women couldn't do them. This was a masculinity based on doing something rather than being something. In losing the public distinctives of masculinity because they are now shared with women there seems to be nowhere for men to go. After all, the private realm of home, nurturing children and intimate friendship is the traditional world of women. Men could become house-husbands but few seem to be convinced.

A society based on a rediscovery of community and connection is a challenge to men. There is no map for them to follow. The challenge is that men seem ill-equipped to make these changes. They have become so isolated from one another and so constrained by the lack of intimacy between men that they find it difficult to form relationships with one another. There is an acute awareness in the men interviewed in this book that they are facing changes which are difficult to define, let alone confront.

Listening to men in these circumstances presents very special challenges. They are not often asked to talk about themselves. It means that we have to learn to listen not only to the words, but the silence and the avoidance, the fumbling for a new language and the desire to divert conversations to conventional male interests. All of these are present in the men interviewed. But what is remarkable in these interviews is the openness of the men to talk about their lives. Even while they say that they find it difficult to express their emotions, they then tell stories and describe experiences which come straight from the heart. They come over as men who not only have a lot to say which is worth hearing but as men who by their words and through their own lives, challenge the stereotypes used of men.

Having said that, one of the problems men face in a world of connection is that they find themselves stifled by a way of relating which seems to demand a lot of words from them about themselves. In such conversations they long to get out into the fresh air to discuss football, work or go down to the pub. But an all-male environment can promote intimacy within the confines of fraternity. It focuses on doing rather than being. The enjoyment of each other's company and the absence of women can bring men into an experience of brotherhood. In environments where men feel safe together different dynamics are found. The football supporter, the soldier in the Marines, or the miner down the pit may all feel close to other men and can be deeply affected by that, but they will have very different means of expressing that closeness. Words are not the only vehicle for intimacy.

All-male environments can be places of amiable competition, a mixture of aggression and humour. There can be physical closeness but little of it is likely to be verbally expressed. On one occasion, when an injured pitman was rescued from a coal mine, there were no words of tenderness or affection even though there was genuine concern at his injuries. Close relationships can change apparent hostility into affection.

But those men who do not work in all-male environments are living in a new kind of society. Even if many men are still uncertain about the future of masculinity they are acutely aware that there is a negative view of masculinity in our culture at the moment. Violence, child abuse, sexual irresponsibility, fraud or lack of public integrity all seem to be laid at the door of men rather than women. The rise in single parent families from one in twelve in 1970 to one in four in 1998 often seems to be attributed to irresponsible male behaviour, and Jack Straw, Home Secretary at the time of writing, has said that the behaviour of young men is the single most serious social problem facing British society. It seems that not only do we have to grapple with a new future as men, but we do it carrying the burden of the past.

The Challenge to Spirituality

Men often go through life keeping their head down hoping that nothing bad will occur. They work hoping that redundancy will not come, that close friends will not die, nor illness lay them low. They leave things unsaid to family. Many have few friends. They internalise pain and grief preserving a face of outward control to the world. Because of this, it is difficult to know whether many of them have something which gives them purpose and meaning, and which says to them, 'This is why you are here.' Of course we all have to carry out the routine tasks at home and work which preserve the functional side of our lives. Yet so many of us are happy to let life go by. As John Lennon said, 'life is what happens when you are making other plans.' Writer Robert Hicks is blunt when he says,

> The saddest men I know are the men who have no real vision for their lives. The man who goes to work every day, comes home, reads the papers, has dinner, watches television and goes to bed – only to repeat the pattern the next day – is not alive or well. Life has been reduced to mere functioning and maintaining.[2]

We find identity through relationships and that is why we will spend so much time in this book looking at them. We start listening to men by asking them about masculinity, by which is meant the expectations, stories and myths through which men interpret what it means to be a man and how they should live in the light of them.

Some are Christians, others are not. They are teachers, probation officers, policemen, chefs, businessmen, journalists or decorators. They are single, divorced, widowed, heterosexual or gay. They are Caucasian, Afro-Caribbean and Asian. Amongst the routines of their lives extraordinary things have happened to them. They talk about themselves and others in a way which is compelling, and they challenge us to listen to them. They also break open the stereotypes about men and force us to fight for a renewed celebration of what it means to be a man.

Celebration?

Some of the men interviewed were uncomfortable with the way in which men were currently perceived. This was one of the reasons why some exchanged the idea of thinking of themselves as men to thinking of themselves as persons. Nathan who was a leader both in his work and in church life said,

> I used to feel guilty – whenever I heard about rape on television, I used to feel angry about that. More than just angry because this had happened to that person, but anger at that and guilt at being a man – at the time a young teenage man.
>
> I really can't say that I can recognise any positives in men. Partly because I see women as being able to lead and make decisions and do all the things that women traditionally aren't allowed to do. I think women are capable of power. If the kind of chauvinist view is that those are men's roles, women should go home – I think that they perform those roles equally as well – what does differentiate [us]? It's not that; it's not about being a leader.

What was positive about being a man for Luke?

> I struggle with that one a bit, really, because a lot of the things that make me feel good about myself aren't about being a man; they are, literally, about being a person, or a person in my current situation, or a person in relationships, or whatever. I can't really think of anything in my life that is really positive,

that is literally based on the fact that I'm a man . . . I suppose the one thing would be that I really like being a father; I really genuinely love being a father. I suppose I'm a man if I'm a father. I suspect if I was a woman I'd enjoy being a mother, but there are certain things about being a father which are different from being a mother. Some of those are things that I don't necessarily agree with, or I find myself getting caught up in, to do with social expectations and things, but it tends to emphasise my role as a father and I'm very happy about that role. So I suppose in that sense that's probably the main thing I see myself as, as a male.

Or as Gordon put it, even if there wasn't anything unique about being a man that wasn't the same as saying that being a man was bad.

I'm not sure that there is anything uniquely good about being a man. Maybe the ability to develop a certain strength physically and that sort of thing, and be physically more able, in terms of average man, average woman. That's about it, as far as I can see. But that makes it sound as if it's bad. But that isn't necessarily so, because I think it's actually quite good to be a man anyway, but it's quite good to be woman . . . It almost feels like a comparative thing and I thought, 'No, it doesn't have to be'. I don't think there's anything particularly unique. I think we have differences and we come at things from different angles and as long as that's respected and perhaps appreciated rather more than it is and with less sense of prejudice, then that doesn't matter.

But Jim didn't have any real perception of himself as a man.

It sometimes comes as a shock to me when people have to think, 'I am a man'. It's just very odd; I don't know why. I don't consciously think of being a particular sex, I don't think.

That may sound strange, but it's not something that's in the forefront of my mind a lot. It's just me. I'm not quite sure. I think until someone says, 'You're a man', or 'This is what men do' – then I might get defensive about it, but . . . not on a day-to-day basis. Unless someone brings it up and then I probably do. But apart from that I don't ponder being male, I don't think.

Asked about common perceptions of men he said:

There's the old cliché about being men, strong, unemotional, uncaring, all those sorts of things. But for the people I know, those are not things that they are. For the men that I know, they are not like that; men aren't uncaring, men have got feelings, men aren't that tough as people think that they are or should be. I think those are the images that are given of men, that's how they should react in certain situations, here's what they should do, this is what they should be doing. The men I know just aren't like that.

    I don't try to be tough because I think that's what men should be. I don't think I try to be uncaring because I don't think that's what men should be. I don't think that I live up to any of the typical stereotypes of what a lot of people think men are. I don't think I try to do that; I wouldn't want to do that either. If that's what people think men are then that's not what I want.

Brian put it like this:

My thing about being a man is a bit like my feelings about being British: it's largely an embarrassment; there's not much about it which I'm very proud of.

But men's roles are changing and with that perceptions of men. This was something on which most had an opinion. Barney said:

I feel I want to get away [from traditional roles] and not treat somebody based upon their sex, but just as a person.

Traditional Men

But far from the conventional role of men having disappeared many readily identified the traditional view of the man as family head and wage earner (the protector/provider/procreator stereotype) and for many this was the place their fathers had occupied. Steve said,

If you think about the way it operated in my family, where it was my dad that worked and Mum was bringing up the kids . . . even the relatives, they all operate in the same way. They've all got their families . . . and they were the providers.

Tony felt that his life on the whole had followed this pattern.

I would always regard myself, and I suppose this undoubtedly comes from my father, as the provider. Although both my wife and I worked . . . I've always taken the role . . . providing parts of our life which I suppose, traditionally, would be expected to come from the man, like security and proper financial arrangements for security.

A serious illness, when his children were very young, had jeopardised this and he had found it very difficult:

It threatened everything, you see, because I had my job; admittedly I hadn't reached any dizzy heights in those days, but nevertheless a fairly responsible job . . . There was the growing family, the job, the mortgage.

Generally, however, he expressed great satisfaction with the way it had worked for his family.

Nick talked of one occasion when he and his wife were very poor,

> I cried. I really wept because I could not provide . . . as a man I was supposed to be the provider.

Paul used the most colourful language in putting over his point of view about being a traditional man,

> If I meet a woman, I feel that I ought to be protective . . . I suppose it goes back to the caveman thing: I'm the one out there; the woman's in the cave lighting the fire and I'm out there killing the ravaging lion. That sort of feel . . . maybe has little to do with what society is saying. Maybe it's something much deeper.

Men in Transition

Sometimes traditional values were passed down from father to son but the actual home situation belied them, causing confusion in the son's mind about whether they were appropriate. This could put his own relationships under strain. Yet the pattern was so powerfully embedded that if it was frustrated relationships could break down. What did Richard think it meant to be a man?

> Whoorgh. I don't know, because in many ways what I was taught it was to be a man when I was a child, or what I learnt, and my view now are totally different things. So what I'd say is that I feel a bit confused about it, to be quite honest. Because I think for me being a man is probably – no, I don't really know. It's a bit confused.

When I was a child, the man was the breadwinner, he was the disciplinarian, he made all the decisions and was basically in charge. That's what society taught us. What I saw at home was slightly different because my mother was in charge, hence my confusion, I think. Now I'm a man myself, . . . – maybe not even now, I don't feel I qualify for that because I don't feel like I'm grown up. So a man is grown up, for one thing. I think it's different things in different environments. If you're talking about men with a relationship to women then – I don't know.

I think my own expectations, then, were that I should be the breadwinner, should be this and should be the other, and that wasn't the life I was leading. So that caused me a lot of conflict. Basically I think it ultimately led to the breakdown of my marriage, because I wasn't fulfilling the role that I thought I should be fulfilling.

But now I've sort of come to the conclusion that that doesn't matter. That role isn't necessarily there. Like, in this new relationship now, there isn't a set, 'This is my role, this is her role'; we do whatever comes along. It's quite fluid and I feel really comfortable with that and I don't feel I've got this role to fulfil. So I think previously it was probably my own expectations, whereas now I take it as it comes. I don't worry about it any more because it doesn't matter.

I think in some ways before it mattered because that was the role we were taught we should have. But I'd seen it not working at home and I know my mother and father aren't happy. Therefore that was because my dad wasn't fulfilling the role he should be fulfilling. So therefore that made him unhappy. So I thought I didn't want to be unhappy so I should fulfil this role. So that was the logic behind it. But now I know it was like distorted logic, so I now don't worry about expectations any more.

Challenging traditional values can be a relief when the man

wants to break away from his upbringing. Michael, who is now retired from teaching, had a traditional upbringing but . . .

I suppose I was brought up with the traditional idea that the man would be automatically the head of the household. This was certainly true for my parents; not, I think, because of any male-domination feeling on the part of my father, but simply because he was a stronger personality and enjoyed better health, for one thing, than my mother, and because, again, he was not only the breadwinner, you might say, the person who earned in the household, but he also controlled the finances and regulated the spending and gave my mother housekeeping money each week and otherwise controlled the family purse strings, if you like.

So that was the sort of background I came from, and I suppose I rather expected that this would be my role. It came as a bit of a shock, I think, when I realised that my wife wanted to be the dominant influence in our family. . . . She was keen to keep an eye on the finances and indeed eventually sort of took over looking over all the family finances. Well, not all the family finances, because I suppose I've still been the person who's done most with regard to income tax forms and investment and that sort of thing, but day-to-day finances she has been happy to take over and I must confess I've been very happy for her to take it over.

But yes, the roles changed then, between the generations, in that certainly I've been quite content, really, to not be the dominant influence in the household. Again, partly because I was too busy, I think, to play this part, it was quite a relief in a way that I didn't have to be making all the decisions about the children; I could leave her to get on with it. She has a strong personality anyway and I think was very ready to take over the more dominant role and although, as I say, it came as a bit of a shock to me to realise that this was really how our marriage was going, in a sense I was relieved that it let me off the hook, shall we say, of having to do all the nitty-gritty of family decision-making and finances that I was really quite glad to be relieved of.

But did he have any particular expectations of what it meant to be a man?

I expect a man to have a stronger physique and I suppose I've always tended to do any of the heavier jobs around the house and garden, for example. I've expected the man to take the initiative, I think, in arranging things like holidays and spare-time activities and (it's a bit difficult to know how to put it) in the personal relationships.

So the model of the traditional man still has a place in men's lives even though they may be moving away from it. The change in roles has happened between the last generation and the current generation, meaning that awareness of the change is psychological and emotional rather than historical as it will be for future generations. The sons of this generation will have a weaker attachment to the model of the traditional male than their fathers. But the new ways of thinking about masculinity do not mean that men have abandoned the acts of providing, procreating and protecting. It is that these acts no longer define the male role but are shared with women. In peacetime the act of protecting is personal but the other roles are still present.

One particularly striking aspect about the interviews was that men described being a man in negative terms related to women. They talked more about 'not being a woman' than about positive male characteristics which could be defined like clear demarcation points on a map. This is usually put down to the need for a man to move away from the mother in order to discover himself as a man. His need at that time is to find a model of being a man which is also nurturing but in a masculine way. If he gets no model or a negative image of masculinity then he may be in difficulties. I talk more about this at the end of the book.

Indeed, one of the most striking features of these interviews was how the men found it difficult to articulate what was positive about being a man even if they felt positive themselves. That does not mean that men cannot celebrate their lives just that they are unsure as to whether they do so in a way which is distinctively masculine. The media is effective at saying what men are not supposed to be like but not at providing an alternative.

Does Masculinity Exist?

Some saw that change had not favoured men. Jerry described this change as a loss:

> Masculinity is all going out the window. Myself, I don't think there is a masculinity now because there's so much of this New Man. New Man might as well be a woman.

Elsewhere, men expressed this lack of a coherent alternative to now unacceptable models of masculinity. Nathan worried that men's needs, physical and emotional, were overlooked:

> I'm confused about what that means, 'to be a real man'. I feel as though society, the media, seems to spend a lot of time and effort addressing women's issues and women's problems, which I think is excellent and necessary . . . It's taken a long time for it to be recognised that men have health problems, men have emotional needs as well.

This focus on women and the lack of a male equivalent to feminism was blamed by Martyn for men continuing to take their lead, their view of themselves, from women:

That's why men are lost, I think, myself as well. We are lost in this thing. Men's attitudes are often dominated by women's attitudes. You are a caring, sharing guy of the nineties, doing the ironing, looking after the kids, and then suddenly you're told, 'Hey! You do that, you're a wimp. I want to go out with a truck driver.'

Along with these indications that perhaps men have lost a sense of identity, there was in several cases anger from individuals who were living a decent life that they were included with other men whom they disapproved of, as though men were a job lot. David was articulate about this. Asked what his view of being a man was, he replied,

I'd answer that first of all by asking you a question, or putting a question back and saying, 'Why is a man necessarily different from a woman?' I'm probably more interested in being an individual, and these are terrible clichés, but being an individual and finding what my potential is and reaching that. So the sex of somebody isn't an issue: for me it doesn't come into it. So I don't have 'a man should be x', but a person should really go for what they're good at and achieve and be all those other clichés in there as well.

I don't know. It's about – for me it's about being a father and having those responsibilities; it's about me being a husband and getting that right; and it's about – just the main elements in my life, really. It's about carrying out work, whatever that may be. However, that view, you see, is actually changing. I'd be quite happy to consider giving up work. I'm not so sure I could just become a house husband, but I'd certainly be happy to give up work and work part-time and do something alongside that. So actually 'a man must work' isn't very strong with me, although I need something, as an individual. I think women need something; it's just an individual thing in terms of what they put into their lives. So I suppose I'd start to try and answer your question by looking at the key elements, or key roles, in my life. Now, whether that's how I view what men should be collectively, I don't know. I'm just into this, that men should be people. I hate the labels.

I'm going to be really honest now. You see, I actually take quite a dislike to men in their traditional stereotypes. So the man that doesn't care too much about his family, or apparently doesn't care too much, so he's always out, or the man who is the big macho, 'I can do anything' man, the man who is disrespectful towards women and messes about, the man who puts other people down, I really have quite a strong view about. So what I might term as the popular or the common view of the male, I actually dislike.

I am aware of being judged sometimes, or – yes, judged – as though I was in that common picture, and that is quite a pressure . . . I think I'm different and therefore I don't want to be lumped in with all those other guys because I am truly living a decent life. So I actually get quite irritated, particularly by ladies who lump me in with other men, and I don't like that and I gently say so, sometimes.

So I am aware of the pressure in that sense, but I don't feel a pressure to become like that. I have no desire to become like that. I sometimes think I wasn't wild enough in my teenage years and perhaps I've missed out somewhere along the line, but I'm happy to be reasonably wild, to be silly at times. So maybe there's an inkling of 'did I miss out on something?' But by and large I'm quite happy with who I am and how I am.

Martyn described heatedly the various sorts of assumptions he felt people might make about him, and expressed his resentment that, by virtue of being a white, male heterosexual, he was held responsible for everything done by white, male heterosexuals in the past:

I am not a potential rapist. I am not a potential child abuser and it really hacks me off. I hate this.

I hate this idea that all men are little boys. That I find most offensive.

Several men felt that they were discriminated against. They thought that there was still an expectation for the father to fulfil the role of provider, and were angry that no provision existed for paternity leave or career breaks for men. Men's contributions to family life were also frequently overlooked.

> In some ways, men with a family are more trapped than a woman who feels trapped at home . . . in terms of how society organises itself. (David)
>
> Men are expected to provide, expected to work hard for the family, so when they can't, they feel small, they feel like they've been pushed into a corner. (Jerry)

Essentially, they were worried that there was a lack of recognition for their position, a lack of approval for their attempts to achieve everything that they felt was expected of them. They were sometimes angry that although they had discarded the old stereotypes, tried to show that they regarded women as equals, and still bore much of the burden of provider, they were unable to escape from this view that, as men, they would always be, at some level, basically unacceptable. They wanted to be seen as individuals, to be given credit for their good points and to work in equal partnerships with women.

As individuals, they could say, 'I'm not like that', and felt angry that this was not recognised, but they were not offering a coherent alternative view of men.

A New Identity?

Men face two dilemmas. Studies show that women are more expressive of emotions such as love, happiness and sadness than men.[3] The inability to express emotion is meant to be characteristic of male roles, but in fact it is dysfunctional. We are all capable of love and of a whole range of human emotions. The problem inexpressive males face is that 'even if they successfully live up to the male role, they suffer adverse consequences.'[4] It seems you can be a 'real' man but only by cutting yourself off from expressing a whole range of human emotions which are not acceptable. A macho man is half a person. The problem expressive men face when compared to traditional males is that they are not considered 'real' men because they express emotions which are considered feminine by 'real' men.

In both models the problem is that insecurity is built in. Whether you are one or the other, you may be missing something. What is needed are secure men who care more about others than about themselves and who believe that relationships with others are more important than personal ambitions. Otherwise how can men become whole without either compromising their emotional life or their masculine identity?

There is a second dilemma for men. If they want to recover a unique masculine identity then they must reclaim some of the ground they at present share with women. Of course many men have never relinquished this ground and view any debate on masculinity with thinly veiled contempt. For them, there is no debate! Those who read this book are betraying the cause! In their view they only have to wait before the fashions change and women go back to the home, this time of their own volition. That will settle it. Men will recover the workplace, their authority, objectivity and control, and women will yet again become the nurturers and caretakers of the home. Why debate? It will all turn out in the end to be too much for them. In the end they will want children and will find they can't have that, a career and a stress-free life. Biology will out in the end.[5]

But fewer women are choosing to have children. Despite the fact that women have always been divided on feminism, the entry of women into the labour market and the financial benefits this has brought to their families as well as to them personally means that this trend cannot easily be reversed, though there is evidence that many women are suffering from stress, especially those who have children. Men find themselves in the situation of wanting to demarcate an area which is their own, while affirming the advances that women have made in recent years. Since it is the entry of women into the market-place which has brought about the demolition of the demarcation of gender roles in the workplace, it does not seem that men can go back to the old days. We are left with celebrating the new flexibility and freedom as if these were incontrovertibly positive.

By adding the world of achievement women have not lost the traditional world of motherhood and home-keeping. Living in both worlds at the same time may cause stress but they continue to co-exist.

Women now drive sports cars bought with high salaries earned through professional excellence. They wear hard hats and manage building sites as civil engineers. They are prison officers, bank managers, barristers and MPs. Women were meant to be intuitive and men rational: now women barristers debate the law in the top courts of the land.

Added to this, the information society does not require physical strength and masculine sweat, it needs intelligence, familiarity with computers and communication skills. The growth of technology is a contributor to changes in men's lives. Manual workers are not needed in such huge numbers and the majority of new jobs, many of them part-time, are going to women. Although in some areas of the workplace women may feel that they are not there in sufficient numbers, that is not the point as far as men are concerned. The change begins when one woman can do the job as well as or better than a man. One woman is all it takes for masculinity to take a hit.

Where can men find the new security they need? Would renewing their spirituality help men to find a new perspective on themselves? Perhaps men will move out of the gender debate into a focus on spirituality because the former cannot bring men to a sense of their own wholeness, whereas the latter can. It is to this possibility that we now turn.

2

Glimpsing a New World

The word 'spiritual' is staging a comeback. Commentators on the arts appearing on late-night television call a film or book 'spiritual' and heads nod wisely. An atheist vehemently denounces those who believe in God but says when asked that she sees herself as 'quite a spiritual person'. What they mean is not clear and perhaps that is the attraction of the word. If it is vague then everybody can use it without having to commit themselves to anything. Labelling oneself 'spiritual' seems a harmless way of deflecting such a criticism while giving off just a hint of mystery. Others see it as a way of convincing themselves that their options are open when it comes to religious faith. It is a form of tolerance of the positions of others who are religious. We are not all as honest as Patrick who said, 'There probably is no meaning to life, I'm probably just a vehicle for DNA to replicate itself.'

It is a word which has not yet settled down. For Ben a spiritual person 'floats in the sky'. But behind the word is the question 'What does it mean to be human?' It is another way of posing the issue of masculinity, but from a different perspective. We are all human beings but from one perspective we are asking, 'What does it mean to be a masculine person?' From the other we are asking, 'What does it mean to be a spiritual person?' Is there any connection between the answers? From a Christian standpoint we are all spiritual people because we are God's creation. If we view ourselves from any other angle we will have a distorted picture of who we are. But we also know that something has gone wrong in us and we need to become whole.

Masculinity is about how the stories, expectations, and behaviour of men are interpreted. As we have seen, for many men masculinity is invisible until a trigger such as a comment or event focuses their attention on that part of their identity. It is no longer possible – if it was ever possible – to talk about masculinity as if there is only one version of it. Each of the men interviewed here has different ways of seeing their lives and we have already become aware of the fact that they feel strongly about being lumped into a homogeneous group rather than having their differences respected. But with men finding it difficult to come to terms with any conscious awareness of their masculinity, it can become a hidden generator of meaning and purpose. It is this which means that listening to men is so important. It is crucial that, because someone else is listening and not interrupting with their own personal agenda, men can hear their own voice speaking. Masculinity is not found in description, it is found in relationship. Listening draws out the uniqueness of each person.

The same is true for spirituality. Many of the men interviewed did not think of themselves as spiritual until someone asked them about it or an event triggered such an issue in their lives. This is not surprising. The word is used so often but in such radically different ways that although we are very familiar with it we are still not sure what it means. It is also true that public and private life are more insulated from religion than in previous generations. In the past it was difficult to avoid religion but now it is relatively easy to confine it to the rituals of life such as confirmation, baptism or marriage without any other commitment to it or even information about it.

Yet in recent years there has been a rush of books on what might be called 'spirituality without Christianity'. Bookshops carry substantial sections entitled 'Mind, Body and Spirit'. Looking at the books in these sections is confusing. At first glance they appear to have very little in common but on closer inspection there seems to be something going on. These books are an alternative to Christianity. They have a very different view of what truth is, and it is this that generates their diversity, while at the same time they are all grouped together under the general heading of 'spiritual'.

Truth is not talked about as a revelation from God, which is the Christian belief, but as what you feel you can believe in. It is not that some things are true whether you believe them or not, but quite the opposite. If you believe them, then they are true for you. The range offered is comprehensive, from witchcraft to meditation, crystals, psychic powers, and various sorts of healing. This is a 'pick and mix' culture. Of course we might expect something like this to happen at the turn of the millennium as we all suffer from a little premillennial tension. The prophets of doom turn out their books as do the prophets of paradise. They fill a space created by the feeling that consumerism is not all it is made out to be. A life spent shopping is not everybody's measure of the deeper life.

We are caught in a trap of our own making. As sociologist Zygmunt Bauman puts it,

> The gap between human needs and individual desires is produced by market domination; this gap is, at the same time, a condition of its reproduction. The market feeds on the unhappiness it generates: the fears, anxieties and the sufferings of personal inadequacy it induces release the consumer behaviour indispensable to its continuation.[1]

So on the one hand spirituality can be a vague addition to a frustrated materialism. On the other hand that very lack of definition has been filled with competing but equally astounding claims which like flowers bloom and fade in a season. In the first sense it is an understatement. Its vagueness is its strength as it can be applied to anything without comment. In the second sense it is an overstatement. It is seen as a empty space just waiting to be filled with the exciting and the bizarre.

But something new *is* happening. There is in people who would not wish to call themselves religious or go within a thousand miles of a church a desire to introduce a spiritual dimension to their lives or to say that there is already a spiritual dimension to their lives.

Men on Spirituality

There seemed to be a lot of agreement on the topic of spirituality, although those men who were Christians had slightly different definitions. Those who were not Christians had a wide variety of comments about what it might mean. Some saw spirituality in terms of being a conventional follower of religion or having moral values, others mentioned being friendly and caring, having guts or having spirit, being open to the world of the spirit, to the unseen, and what you believe in your heart, your 'Soul of souls', your very conscience, your very being.

Dennis said,

I'm a practising Christian; I do attempt to live by Christian ethics. I believe strongly in 'do unto others as you would have them do unto you'. I think if you attempt to be like that in everything you do, I don't think you can do a lot more really. That's where I come from.

I knew someone who was a spiritual man from my point of view, because of how good he was to everyone. He would never do anyone down in any way whatsoever. Whether that relates back to whether it's spirituality that brings that about, or whether that is spirituality, I've got a problem with. I just can't get my mind round it.

I find religion a mystery, can't explain it, have not delved deeply into it. If I did delve deeply into it, I might change my views, and my views are really what I was brought up to understand, rather than what I've put a lot of time in myself thinking through. Because I don't understand; I've accepted but I don't understand. But that doesn't mean to say that I haven't got faith. But if you like it's almost blind faith. I don't know if that makes sense, but that's the situation.

Some men who were not Christians were not sure about whether there was a God or not. They were also not sure about what happened after death. Josh's story illustrates this well:

Years ago I was actually going to go into missionary work . . . But am I agnostic or atheistic or whatever now? . . . In some respects I wish I could believe, because I've known people who do and it clearly has given them great inner peace and all that. So in a sense I'm envious of people who have a genuine belief, whatever it is.

I suppose, yes, I wish I could, wish I could. Is there such a thing? I don't know. I hope to God there is. It would all seem rather pointless if there wasn't. I suppose most of all you like to believe in what's beneath a religion. But I find it difficult to follow some of the ritual.

I haven't gone to church here. Normally where we live, we all go to the church. It's not an inherent religious thing . . . When we used to go to the church . . . we used to enjoy it. We used to go and get some sort of pleasure out of the peace. Without getting into the catechism and all the various bits. I did that when I was at university. All these wonderful religious things that are explained, I'm not into that. I find that all very difficult to follow. Just sort of take that away and say, 'What does religious mean?' Isn't it that on the outside, what they do is good. I'm religious in that sense, or I'd like to be.

I suppose it's not so much that I hope there's a God; I suppose it's much more a hope that I'll meet again the people who I've known who have either died or will die after me . . . I suppose it's more I'd like to think he can just go [clicks fingers] kerplonk. So if Fiona died, I'd like to think, 'Well, I'll just pop and see you again' or vice versa. I suppose it's that; I hope there's something beyond. Because it almost makes a mockery of your feelings for people. Those feelings can be there and very strong and very real, and then finish. The feelings don't finish but the person. That, I think, will always seem rather pointless. But I've no concept of what it looks like.

So I think – maybe that's the cunning part of it – if you didn't feel that there was something, then you could always become very selfish, very short-term, 'Well, I'll make the most of it', and that I think would pander to the worst parts of us, because there are bad parts. So maybe that's the clever bit, that people say, 'Oh well there's something else', and that makes you think, 'I'd better keep myself on the straight and narrow otherwise I'd never achieve it.' If there is, and I hope there is, they'd soon see through that. So my pretending to keep on the straight and narrow just so that I can get on to stage two, they'd soon work that one out:'. . . rumbled you, you bugger'.

Some felt that maybe there was meaning in life, but that maybe there wasn't . . . Mark said:

This is all very complicated and how would this possibly all be here unless there was some sort of meaning to it? But then I have a sneaking suspicion that that's just human beings' way of coping with the fact that we're just here and then we go.

Martyn goes regularly to church but not because he is a Christian:

It gives me time, gives me an hour and a half to collect my thoughts, to divert my mind from something else. I don't look on it as a praise thing. I seldom, if ever, sing hymns, unless it's to myself in the bath. I don't go for the community as such, because I don't know anybody.

. . . I'm still very religious. My religion, however, is some-what egalitarian, in that I believe Christ was the son of God, but on the other hand so was Buddha, so was Mohammed, so are all the other prophets; they were all sons of God.

My God [has] got a sense of humour. He's got faults, like everything, like everyone. But there has to be a plan here. I think of him as forgiving, basically. He's created faults so he has to be forgiving in his self. I don't have this idea of a wizened old guy sitting above the clouds. I can't really explain it; it's an inbuilt feeling, if you like. It's a sensation.

Brian, who didn't believe in God, also described having moments when he was very aware of a spiritual side. He too spoke in terms of a feeling he couldn't put into words. He was brought up as a Christian but has not believed for twenty years.

God is a way of explaining things and is a useful concept . . . but I don't relate to God; I don't have a personal relationship with God: I never did . . . I don't think it's that important to me [involvement in the church]. The values are. And that was what was always important to me, I think.

But equally he seemed to have a hankering after something:

There's something about being on top of a mountain – it's all very romantic tosh probably, but there's something about seeing yourself in the context of the world, or in the context of what religious people would call creation. It's big, and quietness and open spaces, and this is probably nineteenth-century romantic tosh but there is something; there's a feeling about that and I can't put it in words at all . . . it is about quiet, to a large extent, I think.

Oliver has similar views. Although he had a period in his youth when he was a very active (if a bit belligerent!) Christian, in retrospect he feels:

> I forced myself to believe all these things and then went through a crisis of faith.
>
> I've thought about these questions; the big question this year's been, 'What the hell's spirituality?' I've been pondering because it's all been Creationist spirituality, and this, that and the other spirituality. I just keep seeing that word and I haven't got a clue what that one means.
>
> I'm not happy with this idea, the non-conformist biblical idea that if you read St Paul, St Paul says . . . I don't go with that particularly. Well not at all. That's bollocks basically. Where that leaves any roles, I'm not sure.
>
> Going up in the mountains, that was really profound. I don't know what it was but it's that feeling of something beyond you. That's what I'd say spirituality is.

He sees himself as a 'fairly spiritual person' but also says that he is 'fairly earthy'. He's fought shy of what he calls 'this extremist thing' and says,

> I've met people who have got their heads up their backsides as far as spirituality. It's all otherworldly and I don't see spirituality as being that.
>
> Some of the students I work with seem so wrapped up in this selfish bubble that they never seem to see beyond themselves, and I try and fight it with them but that, I think, is spirituality. It's the conquering of that. You can never do it completely but . . . it's conquering that and seeing that there are links that you can make with other people.

Despite many of the ideas of the men interviewed which could be called 'spirituality without religion' (or 'secular spirituality' as I shall call it from now on), a large number of them still saw spirituality in the context of religion. It was as if the two were still connected but that either they were moving in different directions or the word was changing its meaning, becoming 'unhooked' from religion. But several men made no distinction between spirituality and religion, and Jerry was one of these:

> Spirituality I class as in God, as in religion: Catholic, Methodist, Protestant, whatever. Who you believe in. That's what I think spirituality is. I class it as in religion, as in what people think of religion, as in what people think of religion and in what they practise as religion.

He also included alternative medicine, aromatherapists, dowsing, witch doctors and spiritualists in spirituality. But for others it was something which was deeply personal and almost ethereal. Simon said,

> I guess my vision of spirituality is almost a saintliness or a sort of holiness, an awareness – a deep awareness of God within you and your relationship with God, which has a quality about it that is probably evident to other people.

Edward loves the church music which gives him a spiritual experience in terms of awe.

> I've not really thought of any sort of spiritual dimension for such a long time. I suppose whenever I go into a church for a wedding or christening or whatever – there is a sense of awe . . . If I go into a church – not a modern one obviously, not that I've been into one for ages – there's a sense of awe, that people did this out of belief . . . They've been built with love, if that doesn't sound too trite. They've been built for the glory of something. It's been somebody's vision . . . To have done this because they believed in God, not for any other

reason, inspires awe in me . . . but it doesn't make me want to rush up and get baptised. I'm not a Christian.

William Hague, the leader of the Conservative Party, has said a similar thing:

> You don't have to be a regular churchgoer to find peace and spiritual reflection standing in the nave of York Minster or to be profoundly moved by the beauty of choral evensong.[2]

Like Keith, Patrick finds it difficult to believe in the miracles of Jesus. He is an atheist but discusses spirituality with people he meets regularly who are Catholics. He says that increasingly he is a spiritual person.

> I've actually said to people, 'I would love to be a Catholic if I didn't have to believe in God, Jesus, miracles and all the rest of it.'

But like Edward, if there is a heaven, it is through the beauty of choral and religious music (which he loves) that he feels he would get a glimpse of it. For a moment Patrick seems to see choral music as praise or worship, just as those who get a feeling of awe when they walk up a hill are looking at nature as creation, or football fans become congregation rather than crowd when they sing hymns at a cup final. These glimpses of God's handi-work are like small windows which open onto a different world. God is not contained by religion, the whole world is made by him, and if we have gifts – of music or art, hospitality, gardening or football – it is because they are gifts from God to us.

Patrick also talked about spirituality as going beyond or being 'more than' the material or biological. He expressed this by comparing himself to a snail!

> I think it about the bit of me that isn't an animal, really. So

I'm flesh and bones and blood and oxygen and all the rest of it, but it's all the rest of it that I don't quite know, really: why I don't have a shell and leave a slime trail. I'm not a snail, but why I'm me and how I became me and what keeps me as me. I know there are a lot of synapses in my brain that store memories and trigger things and give me speech and sight and hearing and the rest of it, but I'm not sure where that all comes from and actually the sum is more than the parts, I guess, and the sum is probably spirituality, I guess.

So for many of the men spirituality was something beyond them. For some, it was more than the biology of human beings, for others more than beautiful landscape. It was in choral music, in the architecture of the church. It represented a challenge to get out of a restricting selfishness and could produce a very different kind of character. But these things could only be glimpsed from time to time. They were not there on a permanent basis. In fact when attached to human belief or church life spirituality became more of a problem. If we became spiritual, were our motives right? Were we just motivated by the desire to see our now deceased friends again? For others the seeming prerequisite that the spiritual life is only available to those who believe in miracles and the resurrection poses a very real obstacle. Yet the existence of spirituality remains an intriguing possibility.

Prayer as Spirituality

For many of the men prayer was very important. They saw it as a sign of a 'relationship with God' and a conversation with somebody from whom they could keep no secrets. Simon regarded prayer as a very significant part of his life.

It would be interesting, if a fly on the wall followed me during the day, when I'm in the car or walking or going to the shops;

I do tend to pray out loud, I think. Certainly if I'm in the car, for example, whatever comes to mind I do consciously say to God, 'Thank you, Lord, for this', or 'Can you please help me with this situation that's just about to come up?' Which I class as prayer of a sort . . .

Prayer is important. Yes. Particularly when I do actually set myself five, ten, fifteen minutes of prayer; that is not so often nowadays unfortunately. But if there's something I am concerned with, then I do try and get down on my knees or sit down and pray about that. I'm really conscious that if I've covered that area in prayer I can let it go and not worry about it, because I do feel I've given that to God in prayer and I can leave it in his hands, although there are some things which you continue to come back to.

But I strongly believe in the power of prayer and that people and situations do change as a result. But I'm not really the sort of person who prays for a parking space. (I probably have done; I'm sure I do pray for all sort of trivial things like that as well . . .)

Some had a regular prayer life in which they prayed for their families and for other people. Others prayed less regularly but wanted to pray more. Prayer was about relationship or knowing God. It confirmed that those men who were Christians saw their religion in terms of a divine relationship which, like any other relationship, could grow and get deeper. They also expected something to happened as a result of prayer. Some commented that prayer changes the world. Others observed that prayer had changed their lives. Theodore Zeldin's description of the art of conversation is perhaps one of the best analogies of prayer:

The kind of conversation I'm interested in is one which you start with a willingness to emerge a slightly different person. It is always an experiment, whose results are never guaranteed.

It involves risk. It's an adventure in which we agree to cook the world together and make it taste less bitter.[3]

Errol was somebody who now saw prayer as conversation,

> Prayer: fundamental in my life. Brought up in a Christian home, where prayer has always been top of the agenda, through family worship, through Sunday School and church, and even now prayer is an essential element, at night, in the mornings. Not mainly petitioning[4] God, but actually – the more I get older, it's a move away from petition; it's trying to get more conversational and trying to, sometimes, reason, which I find difficult. I don't understand things, a lot of things, but I'm getting more patient in my prayer life. Before it was – I had a list of things that I wanted to say, but now I'm giving more time to reflection.

Worship – the coming together of Christians to praise and adore God – was obviously important to some.

> I see worship as something that says to the world, 'This is God's space, this is God's people,' because I look at worship as people coming together to be with God but not to be unaware of what's outside in the world. Like stones looking outwards rather than stones looking inwards to the church. The church is a building looking outwards, not inwards.

Chris brings us up sharp and reminds us that not everyone finds prayer, worship and spirituality helpful. His comments were stark and uncompromising.

> prayer . . . that just has religious overtones for me and where there is nothing against religion per se, I don't think religion has ever done any good. It's just made people kill more people, basically. So I don't really think much about prayer. That's not

to say that I don't believe in anything but what I believe in is personal dignity and how you relate to other people. You give them respect, you expect it yourself.

Despite the difficulties of nailing down the idea of spirituality outside the treatment of it by a particular religion, it did mean something to the men interviewed and often something important, whether or not they could put their finger on it. Both Christians and non-Christians associated it with the way they lived their lives. Many men spoke about the human heart when they spoke about spirituality. They spoke of: a searching thing, a journey; the very core of me; something that's at the centre of me that affects the way I operate within my relationships; the greatest honour a person could have (to be called spiritual); a pride in things beyond you; a relationship with God.

Why is prayer another important point where masculinity and spirituality meet? It signifies the willingness to consider giving up control of your life. Men like to be in control of their lives but prayer properly understood and practised as a way of life is the exact opposite of that point of view. If there is a God who listens then it makes sense to give control over to him. If God is not there, don't bother praying, go and have another drink. Control is about the visible and the definable, but God is neither visible nor definable. Relationship with God is an act of faith as is prayer. So prayer is not about a shopping list, it is about being obedient to the will of another. Ironically within Christianity it is this idea that provides the basis of freedom, as one does not carry around the burden of being the arbiter of one's own destiny. It could be called something like 'the freedom of obedience' and is a radical step away from contemporary lifestyle and especially masculinity. If spirituality is about freedom then prayer is an essential part of men rediscovering the soul.

Crowd as Congregation

Several of the men related spirituality, passion or motivation to football. Barry and Martyn certainly did.

Now we're talking football! I suppose I feel very passionate about my wife. I feel very passionate about my kids. I feel very passionate about life, in terms of enjoyment.

The things I feel really passionately about are my children . . . Next comes my partner, next comes cooking. And I'm very passionate about . . . football.

Oliver was somebody who saw football as a spiritual experience.

I've had spiritual experiences down at the city ground. One night against Derby, when Roy Keane played on the wing, he actually played a blinder and I felt, 'I'm just proud of you for playing like that' . . . I think that's what spirituality is, for me anyway, it's pride in things beyond you.

So what is it about football that can make him 'shed tears of joy'? Simon tried to explain:

Just the excitement when the team scores a winning goal in the last minute or achieves promotion or something like that is a sort of high that you don't match in any other sphere of life, to be honest. It might be momentary, and conversely disappointments can be equally low. For men, it provides a range of emotions that are not experienced in any other form of life.

It has often been said that football is a religion. Those for whom football is important say that being a football supporter is a fundamental expression of something deep within them. Football is a safe environment for men, a talking point with other men and it provides a sense of identity. It's not just about watching an enjoyable game, it's full of tension, expectation and passion.

When Brian was told about the interview he thought, 'I bet we talk about football'. So, what is it about football?

I honestly don't know. What is it I enjoy? Part of it is a lad's day out sort of thing. It's an event going to the match and then going to the pub afterwards, although I don't stay that long, and meeting up with three of four people . . . We've been sitting in the same seats for ages and it's the only time I see them really – match days.

But there is something inherent about the football, I suppose. What I was thinking is that it's the expectation of the scoring of goals. I'm not into all the technicalities; it's something about being able to leap out of one's seat and punch the air and shout, 'Yes'!! It's something that gets you out of yourself, I suppose. It's the expectation of that rather than watching some nice pretty patterns on the pitch, I think that's what I get out of it . . . It's not losing myself in a mass of people or anything, because we call the people who sit around us 'the living dead' and the others, that aren't the living dead, tend to boo the team rather than cheer them.

Watching football is an activity which seems to give many men their primary sense of meaning, community, identity and emotional expression. For some it gets them out of difficult relationships at home, and gives them a few hours of space to themselves. Watching football is a community thing but it is also something 'just for me'.

But many of the men interviewed included it, alongside loutish behaviour and getting drunk, in their characterisation of the kind of man they didn't want to be. These kinds of attitudes served further to emphasise the importance of football as a touchstone of masculine identity, whether men liked it or not.

Football and competitive sports generally have often been

said to be a replacement for war, appealing to the innate warrior instinct in every man. (Perhaps one of the problems with religion is that it does not have this same attraction for the warrior instinct.) None other than Malcolm Allison, the British football manager, has said, 'Professional football is no longer a game. It's a war. And it brings out the same primitive instincts that go back thousands of years.'[5]

Winning and being defeated, competing, identifying, and having heroes are all common elements between sport and war. In the nineteenth century the language of the battlefield and of sport (particularly athletics) were inextricably intertwined, with the epithets of self-sacrifice pervading both. Sport was seen as a way of developing moral character. Its heroes were appropriate models for young men.

For committed supporters, football is not just about belonging to a group for those few moments on a Saturday afternoon, though it is that. It is also about being able to express both celebration and tragedy. It takes a morally innocuous occupation and gives it some of the power others might express through religious worship, music, art or poetry. For a few minutes thousands of men move from being 'crowd' to 'congregation'. They even sing hymns, especially at prestigious games such as the cup final. In defeat or in victory there is no shame in a man weeping at a football game.

Nick Hornby demonstrates the importance of football as something with which men not only identify in their lives but even in their deaths.

I do not want to die in mid-season but on the other hand, I am one of those who would, I think, be happy to have my ashes scattered over Highbury pitch (although I understand there are restrictions: too many widows contact the club, and there are fears that the turf would not respond kindly to the contents of urn after urn). It would be nice to think that I could hang around the stadium in some form, and watch the first team one Saturday, the reserves the next; I would like to feel that my children and grandchildren will be Arsenal fans and that I could watch with them. It doesn't seem a bad way to spend eternity, and certainly I'd rather be sprinkled over the East Stand than dumped into the Atlantic or left up some mountain.[6]

3

Why Bother with Religion?

Something is happening in the world of religion. The number of people who are churchgoers is decreasing while the interest in spirituality is increasing. In one sense we have never been so religious. As we have seen men do not necessarily see the church as the natural place to help them on a spiritual journey. A divide is opening up between the spiritual life and church life. There are exceptions to this in the popular evangelical and 'charismatic' churches where there is a strong emphasis on spirituality within the church and help for people with their personal life outside the church. But they too are facing the same problems with which Western culture is grappling.

Perhaps it is only fair to remember that membership of all kinds of institutions is on the decline, such as trade unions; so this problem is not confined to the Church. We are all with-drawing from public commitments, preferring to stay at home. Perhaps this apparent divide between spirituality and religion is due to the fact that they have different ways of approaching life. Secular spirituality sees itself as composed of questions. To ask a question is honest. To doubt is also a sign of openness and a sign of our common predicament with others. But from that perspective Christian religious belief is seen as approaching life from the opposite direction. It offers answers. This approach is seen as stopping the freedom to ask questions. Surely, they say, this is dogmatism at its worst? How can any person possibly know that what he or she believes is true for everybody? It is one thing to say that something is true for you but to insist it must be true for everybody is an act of oppression. You are setting yourself up as an authority over others against the free spirit of enquiry which we at the end of the twentieth century regard ourselves as possessing. 'A Sunday school teacher asks his class: "what little grey animal climbs trees, gathers nuts and has a long bushy tail?" A little boy answers: "I know the answer is supposed to be Jesus or God but it sounds like a squirrel to me." '[1] From this perspective religion is seen as closing down the spiritual quest because it may not encourage questioning, only asking people to listen to the answers. However, for the Church, the problem with the concept of pilgrimage as perpetual questioning is that the answers to the questions can never be found, and so, 'secular spirituality' is not only fuelled by discontent but perpetuates discontent.

Of course the Church can forget creativity, becoming lazy in its certainties. It can forget that, for many, life is about paradox and replace the mysteries of life and God with a dry rationalism posing as coherence. It can marginalise people who don't fit in with the Church, preferring irrelevance to discomfort. It is amazing that the Church has survived so long. If it was a firm it would have gone into liquidation in the first century. Thankfully the Church is not God, even though there are plenty of Church leaders who think they are God. But the Church is composed not of people who have arrived but of people who have begun a journey. They are not setting themselves up as those who know all the answers, but are themselves discovering that there are answers to be found. They are those who believe that, even if we feel alone in the world, we are not. In doing so they continue to make many mistakes as they always have done.

Relating to the Church

When talking about religion and the difference between spirituality and religion, it was the church which seemed for many of the men to signify the presence of religion. Spirituality (whether Christian or secular) was seen as a personal thing. Religion was an institutional thing. So it's important to look at men's experiences of the church before we go any further.

In more than one case the church played a part in supporting men when they were in need. Several of the men had faced harrowing experiences forcing them to ask fundamental questions about life. John's story illustrates how this not only renewed his faith but made him feel that he needed to belong to a church community for support and encouragement. The cause of this was the tragedy of a still-born child.

> . . . when I saw him born, the feeling was that I would chop my right arm off to see him breathe. It absolutely blew me away . . . nothing else seemed to have any value except life and the people you are involved with.

It was this that eventually led him to recognise his dependence on God and to say to God,

> 'Look, none of this makes any sense to me. I can't cope with it, no matter what I try and do, no matter which way I move, something blocks it or somebody moves in a different direction.' In the end it came to being reduced to my knees and saying, 'I cannot cope with this any more, please help', and I gave it over to him.
>
> I hadn't even looked at the church. I'd continued to pray on my own, continued to value my perception of the love God has, Jesus has, for us, which seemed in conflict with the church as it was.

John started by going to church services and then began to find peace and calm through both the services and the help he received from the pastor. Eventually he became very involved in its activities. But this was only the first of several tragedies in his life. What did spirituality mean for John?

> Well, to me it's just the very core of me. It's the something that is at the very centre of me that affects the way I operate my relationships with people and with the community as a whole. . . . It's there, I hope, in everything I do.

Ben was one of those who were Christian believers but not churchgoers.

> I was brought up in the C of E and I've been confirmed. I'm quite comfortable about Christianity. I'm not a churchgoer but I lead prayers every day. Every time I do assembly, I tell a prayer and I don't feel hypocritical. I believe in what I'm saying. I would consider myself a Christian, but then people, some people say you can't be a Christian if you don't go to church, which I think is crap if you don't mind me saying so, because I know some regular churchgoers who are not particularly nice people. So I don't think you can say that Christians, that good people go to church and bad people don't. That's silly.
>
> I do believe – I don't pray every day or anything like that, but I sometimes have a prayer in my head. Then sometimes I think, hang on a minute, I'm only doing this because I need a bit of help. But then that doesn't bother me either because I think it's nice to talk to somebody – a friend in need and all that sort of thing.

But does he think he's a spiritual person?

> Am I a spiritual person? I think about the way I treat people

and I think about the right and wrong. I consider the morality of issues. In that sense I suppose I'm spiritual. But there is an idea that being spiritual means floating on a cloud. I don't have an aura. I don't think when I'm in a cocktail bar people gravitate towards me. I don't think in that sense. I'm not Uri Geller. I can't make spoons bend. But I like to think I'm a thoughtful person about the way I behave.

Objections to the Church

Some of the men interviewed had gone through experiences which had caused them to react sharply to Christianity as reflected in the life of the Church. Often this was expressed as an apparent contradiction between the claims of Christianity and the way the Church inadequately expresses those claims or even blatantly contradicts them by its actions. The two stories below illustrate these reactions. In the case of Barney it was his upbringing in a religious context which he found oppressive.

Barney was brought up with a religious background. He described his father and mother as 'non-practising Christians' from different denominational backgrounds. They thought going to church was the right thing to do so they went as a family until his early teens. He went to a very strict Catholic all-boys school. He rejected the competitive values that went along with the rest of the culture and was aware that his reaction against that part of his life was even more important than the influence of his parents. He characterised Catholics as either being

very devout or quite angry and negative about it, which is certainly the effect it had on me.

It's probably tied in, as much as anything else, to do with my own personality. Everything had to be so accepting; you were not encouraged to question anything at all. There's an element of faith, blind faith or whatever you want to call it, in any religion, but it's always struck me that with the Catholic Church it's much more absolute . . . it's almost heresy to question things . . . I've very little respect for it . . . if anything I think it's a negative force in the world. Obviously . . . you are going to have plenty of essentially good people who believe in that particular form of Christianity for very good reasons, and they will be doing a lot of good, but if you are talking about the Church as an institution. No.

David was brought up in a Christian home with a strong commitment to the Church. As he got older he began to have difficulties reconciling life with faith. At a certain point in his life he decided to rethink. As a result he and his family left the Church. Now he sees himself as 'far less spiritual in a traditional sense than I ever have been'. He talked this move through with his parents who were upset. But now he feels he is left with a blank sheet of paper. Although he meets occasionally with a group of like-minded people he says he is beginning to drift:

> And now . . . I am trying to think, 'What do I believe, what is spirituality about, who is God, what is church about, what are these Christians about?' And I was one of them . . . But I haven't thrown out God . . . I hope to get back to a better understanding of God.
>
> I've now got a blank sheet of paper. I've actually thrown everything out to then put back in the bits that I'm happy with and work on the other bits. I haven't found that easy. That has been tremendously difficult because it's gone against everything I've ever known; it's gone against my parents; it's gone against my parents-in-law; it's gone against friends . . . some people have actually completely chopped us off and have been antagonistic, which is not an easy thing. We feel quite alone now and lonely. You've just lost a whole family, so that's not an easy place to be. I think it's quite a brave thing that we've done.

The Church offers, 'This is what the Bible says. This is what you need to believe. Feel guilty if you don't believe it, and please don't ask any questions because that's a bit uncomfortable.' And I don't fit into that now . . . What I would like is to be here and to sit and chat things over with somebody who is prepared for me to say outrageous things and then talk it through with me. We've not found a forum that does that and we feel alone.

I was coming out of church thinking, 'What the heck has that got to do with my life? Where was any of that of any use? God doesn't want what I've just listened to, I'm sure.' What he wants is my better interaction with you, my better interaction with the kids, my wife, the people at work. It's about being in the world and I think we've got so hooked up onto what Jesus said and, 'Let's get it right and if you don't get down on your knees and pray about it' that we've lost being – I'm getting all passionate now, you see. I think the Church can be so vital and relevant, and I think what Jesus was saying was something completely different, far more refreshing, far more vital to how we might exist today. Far more relevant.

We are encouraged from an early age to ask questions of others and to be willing to be asked questions and defend our answers. The importance of being able to ask questions is not just a feature of Christianity. Ahmed found the teaching at the mosque difficult to get on with,

I mean, going to the mosque when I was younger, I'd loved to have asked questions. I don't believe in doing a religion if you can't question it. What's the point in it? If you're just told, 'This is how it is and you've got to believe this', you can't question it because it was written in stone. There's no growth in it, is there?

It is difficult for people who are used to learning by investigation to be asked to accept teaching without being given an opportunity to question. Indeed this is part of a much bigger problem about the way we communicate as Christians. The point was also made by Prof. Steve Jones, Professor of Genetics at University College, London, in an interview.

> I know a number of religious people, with whom I have no quarrel at all. But what I do find galling, I have to say, is people who are religious and can't take criticism; and that often happens. They're perfectly willing to attack me, so they should expect to be attacked themselves . . . It's the inability to be willing to be proved wrong that I dislike about the whole religious argument[2]

Luke doesn't have many Christian friends for the same kind of reason. It is difficult to have open conversations with them.

> I don't have any close friends who are Christians, who I would sit and talk to. I find, by-and-large, most people who adopt major religions, you always hit a problem when you get to the point where you're willing to consider most things in an open way but they feel bound by their own dogma not to question certain things, because it would then, in effect, stop them being who they say they are within that religion. So I find that quite difficult. So not many Christians, really.
>
> Even if God is everything he's supposed to be in the Bible and he created everything, well – it's a bit like me saying to my kids, as it were, a rough analogy, 'I am your dad and because I'm your dad you have to do everything I say'. To me the two don't correspond. They have every right to question me and I feel we have every right to question other things.

This issue of being able to ask questions seems to be an important feature of the attitude of men to religion. They are not willing to take things on trust, but want to satisfy themselves by questioning.

This is also fundamental to the Church's integrity. If it claims to have the truth then it should not be afraid of any question. Nor should it be afraid of admitting when there are no answers. The more dogmatic the Church is the more it loses its authority in the contemporary world. Yet it is also essential that the Church stands by its historic beliefs. Far from backing down on them it needs to be confident about the Christian faith.

In society today we decide what is 'right for us' and express it in terms of our personal integrity. So someone may say, 'If I said I believed in the miracles of Jesus I would lose my personal integrity'; or 'I cannot with integrity believe in hell'; 'If I want to find my own way then that is up to me. After all it is me that has to stand before God, if he exists, and give account of myself. I must be happy with what I believe'. This 'patchwork spirituality', in which we put together those elements of the Christian faith with which we are happy, is a fundamental challenge to the coherence of religion. We are looting it for the bits that take our fancy. No wonder we then criticise it for not making any sense.

In terms of Christian belief the further individuals stray from Christian teaching the greater the danger that their view of God will mutate. One of the functions of the Church is to remind us of the truth about God. Alongside the 'patchwork faith' phenomenon there exists the danger of the 'lottery God': the worship of a God who does what we want him to do. 'Find me a parking space' or 'Give me the right numbers for the lottery, God'!

Dennis felt that 'organised religion' was important.

Well it does help me because the organisation, the discipline, if you like, if that wasn't there I think I could drift away from Christianity altogether and become agnostic. I think I need the discipline aspect to keep me involved.

Gordon who came out as gay some years ago had strong opinions about the Church. He was brought up in the Catholic tradition, served as an altar boy and was involved in the life of the church. Now he is disappointed with it.

I can't believe that established religion can be so oppressive when Christ wasn't. I just find it totally an anathema. I used to consider the Church to be, not quite left of Lenin, but radical, to have radical policies and radical ideas and to believe in the equality of individuals, because that was the sort of background I was brought up in.

I think once you stand outside the Church, or the Church pushes you out, potentially – the Catholic Church would claim not to, but it would probably refuse me communion if I walked up to the altar with 'I'm glad to be gay' on the front of my T-shirt. They would refuse me communion. That I find to be absolutely, totally a hypocrisy. If God is love and he made me, he made me to love another man and that's exactly what I do. If the Church can't handle that, then I think it needs to look to its fundamental principles and not all the add-ons and bits and pieces that it's acquired on the way through. I know full well that the established Churches had – or it would have been *the* established Church, in other words Roman Catholicism – did actually have same-sex marriage ceremonies and partnership ceremonies and blessings, but they were quietly tucked away and hidden, like 'Oh, can't have that'. You get one homophobe who thinks it's wrong, or has a bad experience, just somebody who has a bad experience, who then talks to other people who have a bad experience, who then gang up and produce witch hunts. The term 'faggot' comes from burning, from men chucked into the fire to help the witches burn, and the witches were very often lesbians.

So the established Churches . . . – I don't think they need to go back and be fundamentalist or anything like that; what I think they need to look to is their true principles and to be much more Christ-like, because I don't think they are at all.

[I'm talking about something which is of longer standing

52

than since I came out.] I think that there were other experiences to do with the way that churches are organised, to do with congregations and people within them and the way in which those congregations are, or can be, self-serving rather than serving the church, which I think can be dodgy in a sense, but certainly not putting the Christ part of it – and that's my worry. And that was my worry – I just felt these people seemed to be back-slapping and self-serving and moving up the ladder in order to gratify themselves and that wasn't what I was taught. That's coming from a Roman Catholic background. That was not how I was brought up to believe. And this was somebody who used to go to church twice on Sundays and every morning; as an altar boy you did it. And I even considered the priesthood at one stage. Glad I didn't. Even more hypocrisy.

I do believe in God. Mm, yes, I do. I do. He sometimes fails me, but I still do. I also pray. And it isn't just as I've got older, nor is it like childhood prayers by the bedside. I've gone into church and I've said it, 'Please take this away from me; I don't want to be gay, etc. etc.' And then said, 'Look okay, if that's what's going to happen, if this is who I am, teach me how to be the best person I can be.'

Ahmed comes from a very close and loving Muslim family. His father and he had confrontations as his father was keen to teach him about Islam and he resisted. When he was little he was taken to the mosque and was left there, scared to speak because he didn't know what was being said.

For my dad it's just for show. He just wanted me to be there for people to say, 'Oh, his son is here', which I don't see the purpose in. And today he says, 'Why don't you come down to the mosque?' Well, what's the point in me coming to the mosque? What is the point? It looks good for you. I think they've got this thing where if you get people to go to the mosque, you get points from God or something or it's considered good.

Despite some hard and painful clashes with his father in childhood and as a young man, Ahmed has respect for him and remembers some good times.

> I don't really feel close to him, but I know he's got some really good things about him, because at one point, when I was feeling, really, really bad, he put his arm round me and said, 'It doesn't matter'. And I just thought, 'Wow, that's great.' We don't have many moments like that, and it takes extreme things to happen for it to be brought out, but I know it's there.

The Life-Cycle Needs of Men

Men have different spiritual needs throughout the life-cycle. Like walking around a statue they see life and faith from different angles. A group of retired men anticipating twenty or more years of healthy living are facing issues which have not yet occurred to the young twenty-year-old who probably thinks that anybody over thirty is ancient and sees things in black and white.

As one interviewee explained,

> As this arrogant kid in his mid- to late-teens, I was able to analyse things in a way which young people can – very black and white, obviously. And also think quickly – your brain is very active at that age. That was a time when I couldn't find anything spiritual, any truth, in what I saw around in church.

Of course some of the younger men interviewed already had families which meant that they could not just think of themselves or, if they did, they bore the costs of doing so. They were the 'jugglers' who tried to combine ambition with the family. In other cases men were facing the enormous challenge of trying to combine redundancy with family. Many of those who write and speak on masculine spirituality speak of the male life-cycle and of its importance both in terms of masculine identity and of Christian spirituality. Men have marked patterns of ascent and descent throughout their lives.

Young men have a great deal of energy in their lives. They want to make something of themselves and conquer the world. They head for the top. Their energy is focused. They are continually testing the limits under which they currently operate. Self-control is essential to them. If they are not in control of their own destiny then they cannot reach their objectives. What was Jim's driving force?

I suppose ambition, to be the best of what I can be, is definitely quite a strong driving force for me.

The energy of young people is essential to any healthy society, to families and to their own sense of well-being. It is a gift to the community. Out of it comes the fruit of creativity and innovation. These men are positive and have not yet faced a life crisis. However, such young men are in constant danger. Unless they have spiritual resources they may find that in later life they cannot face periods when things go wrong. Josh commented,

Success is very, very important. I work with some people who are very young and very bright, frighteningly young and frighteningly bright. They have this enormous talent – they're asleep with more than I've got – but at the same time there is this great ambition within them . . . But that ambition sort of twists them. So perhaps as you get slightly older, perhaps the best thing about life is to become less twisted in your ambition; because it can twist.

Nathan sounded a note of caution, knowing there may be costs, because he already had family responsibilities,

> I am ambitious and I am aware of my potential. I am also aware of how that possibly conflicts, maybe increasingly so, as my ambition hopefully begins to be realised, will conflict more with other life goals like being a good husband and time for Veronica and me, and in due course a family.

Did he have anxieties about the future?

> Yes, I do. I have anxieties relating to ambition and will I realise that potential, will I fail?

In that case perhaps Jim was in a safer position!

> I've got no particular goal other than to hopefully grow old and die gracefully.

For men in their mid-life the momentum has usually slowed down. If men's lives are in the shape of a hill then young men use their energy to climb, and mid-life is a plateau before the descent of the hill in older age. Those in mid-life are often facing a crisis of meaning in their lives. Earlier in their lives they may have wanted a good wage, status or power, but now they may want meaning or to make a contribution of some sort to the community. Luke makes the point:

> But my main interest . . . over recent years has been learning more about myself . . . It's about saying (and I think there's a little bit also about being very loosely middle-aged, in the very true sense of the word 'middle-aged'), 'Well I don't want to acquire lots of shiny things, I don't want to be powerful, I don't want a bigger house, a bigger car. I'd actually like to reduce the number of physical, external objects that clutter

my life and concentrate more on understanding who I am
and where I fit into it all and how I can make the best of the
rest of my life, in a personal sense . . . I don't ever think I'll get
there. But I think the whole point is that you travel; that's the
whole idea. As you go along . . . you learn more about
yourself. I do generally feel that; I'm not just saying that
because this is about spirituality. This is what I'm after.

Of course a man may never ascend but may be born into
disadvantage, and never given the start in life he wants. Very
early on in his life he asks the question, 'What is this all about?'
He needs mentors and a community of support and friendships
if he is to survive intact. But out of that experience can come
somebody who is determined to rise above his problems. Far
from succumbing to despair such individuals use the energy of
youth to overcome. As these men have shown, problems can hit
at any time in a person's life. But for those who have been
ascenders there will in mid-life be a sense of disappointment as
problems begin. Younger people overtake us at work, friends
become ill, divorces take place, anxiety breaks out.

Charles had problems when he was threatened with
redundancy,

My first wife said I went 'funny' when I was threatened with
redundancy. I think I did. I think during this period of
uncertainty not so long ago, where the retirement option
wasn't around and I saw what I do here was undergoing major
change and it wasn't a change that I think I welcomed. I was
uncertain whether I wanted to and whether I could even if I
did want to. That certainly resulted in . . . high blood pressure
and so on.

The problem with today's men is that because they try to
maintain control, they often have to hit a crisis in their lives
before they will take stock. A life-threatening accident,

redundancy, divorce, illness: all these experiences may stop men in their tracks and enable them to see that the course they have set themselves on may be self-destructive. In spiritual terms they have been leading an 'unexamined life'. It has been momentum which has given them meaning and this has enabled them to ignore not only their spiritual condition but also their health and their family.

The examined life on the other hand is the life of the man who is spiritually tuned in to the four relationships: God, soul, others, work. Prayer, reflection, listening, spiritual discipline all enable such a man to lead a 'paced life'. Instead of burdens such as guilt, anxiety, shame or resentment building up inside him until they burst like an overloaded dam, they can be dealt with one day at a time. The lessons of the examined life are a principal way in which mid-lifers not only find meaning for themselves now, but also deal with any sense of failure about the past.

Men in mid-life often enjoy men's groups because they are open to share with and listen to others who are at the same stage of life as them. Put them in a group with men from different stages of life and it will not work as well. Such groups are not the same as men's meetings, but constitute small groups where men can come and find friendship together on any basis they want.

In mid-life those things which were definable and seemed black and white throughout men's younger lives, now become paradoxical. Theories about the nature of suffering become distressing and urgent as suffering begins to intrude on life. Some of the rules they lived by don't seem to work any more. The idea of controlling life begins to slip as things happen over which they have no control. Mid-life may be the time when after taking stock we decide to change something in our lives. Barney talked about this in terms of wanting to move from a secure well-paid job to something less-well paid but more creative,

[it's] certainly a lot more risky in terms of prospects and what have you. I suppose a bit of a mini mid-life crisis. I thought, 'Well, here I am in my mid-thirties and I still haven't done what I always said I really wanted to do. Go and do it, for better or for worse. See what happens.

It is difficult to accept that it is at this kind of time that the call to spiritual pilgrimage is at its most insistent. Here is a chance to change the basis of the way we live our lives. The examples of this from the Bible are many and the message is still that in order to grow spiritually we have to give up control. When Abraham was told by God that he was to move from his home and neighbourhood to a life which God would show him he was moving from certainty to uncertainty and from control to faith. This move is an essential part of the spiritual life. He was pretty old when he set out.

If in mid-life we make that change then the period of descent which follows is not a negative thing. Of course it is something which happens to every man. As retirement and old age approach the question of mid-life, 'What should I do with the rest of my life?', turns into, 'What have I done with my life?' Do we have wisdom to pass on to the next generation and a richness of spirit ourselves, or are we dried-up old fools who did not see life as a spiritual pilgrimage?

Those who wish to live a spiritual life must come to terms with suffering. Suffering is a significant though unwelcome part of our lives. Without it the perspective of our lives may be distracted by all those things which are unimportant. The sufferings of mid-life as well as the disappointments pose a tacit question: Are your priorities still the same? To harden ourselves to say yes, rather than to be willing to reconsider, is to miss out on the growth of manhood. For Christian men the aim of life is to become like Christ. This is an aim which we will never fully attain but it sets the direction of our lives. All these experiences are part of that journey.

As we become elderly and face retirement, and ask ourselves

how we are going to spend it, it may be that spirituality becomes more important to us. Charles spoke of his desire to look forward to the next twenty years as a retired man but he didn't know what he was going to do with them:

> I'm certainly going through a major change – not particularly turmoil, though there is some turmoil – a major change of gear into what I'm going to do for another little under twenty years, which has to do with job change, and now it would seem, a family change, forced on me. I guess that spiritual things will become more important as I have the opportunity – as I have the opportunity and the willingness – to engage them.

This analysis depends on men being secure enough to be insecure, which is what Christian spirituality is about. Believing that God is there and is trustworthy enables us to let go of the material world. Spirituality is about what we desire: what we want from life for ourselves. The other side of the coin is that if we desire God we must let go of everything else.

This kind of analysis is now familiar in the writings of those who focus on masculine spirituality and is most associated with Richard Rohr. It is helpful not only for us to see that the masculine journey mirrors the spiritual journey, but that people need to hear those messages which are appropriate to the context of their lives. The question is, how does the Church respond to the life-cycle of men? Men need more than meetings. They also need to be challenged and encouraged spiritually. If the Church does not teach young people and lay the foundation for the rest of their lives then their lives may fall apart when they come under pressure. If the Church does not allow people to ask questions and to challenge its teaching they may leave because the Church, ironically, has become irrelevant to their spiritual journey. This could be either because it defines it too narrowly or because it asserts it too dogmatically.

In summary, then, the spiritual and religious needs of men vary according to the stage of life they are at, the public or private nature of religion, the relevance of the Church, the context in which they are living their lives, or to crises which occur in their lives. Yet again the two agendas of spirituality and gender cannot be separated because they are both fundamental expressions of our humanity.

The Relevance of Preaching

Several men including David mentioned that they found the doctrinal aspects of the Church difficult or the preaching disconnected from their lives. A recent survey agrees.[3] Out of 400 evangelical churchgoers 50 per cent said the preaching and teaching was marked by lack of relevance, depth and challenge. The position was even worse when scored on 'helpfulness'. Out of a possible mark of 4, work was an abysmal 1.7, Home 1.8, Church 2.1, Personal 2.6. Fifty per cent of the people surveyed had never heard a sermon on work.

This is also part of the mix. One of the reasons why men are not in the churches is that the Church isn't relevant to their lives. They live in a community of work, work out their identity at work, face most of their ethical crises at work, and many spend more time at work than at home. Yet the Church seems to be disinterested in work preferring to either talk about the Church or address people personally and in a private context. This approach not only cuts out huge chunks of any Christian message but ensures that those whose primary identity is as workers will be quietly slumbering in the pews. Sermons can be technically brilliant but the application, which takes up a minute at the end, is often simplistic.

Celebrating the Church

Although many of the men who were not Christians had negative comments to make about the Church, there were a few who did have admiration for some people within it. Luke was one of these.

> In mainstream Christianity, I suppose the only thing that draws me towards it in any way is that I do have a very great respect for the Christians who are actually what I would call 'Christian' in the sense of those who actively live their faith and genuinely act their faith out. And I suppose I respect the Quakers, I respect the Sally Army, I respect people like some of the groups who are basing themselves on [them[, elements of the Catholic, or even the Church of England, who are doing social programmes, because I feel what they're doing is taking that kind of edict of love being the main thing and they're actually enacting it. I'm drawn to them in the sense that I respect them and I appreciate what they do and I would happily work alongside them, but it doesn't make me want to join them or become part of that same group.

For some of the men interviewed the church was a place they were able to use their gifts and serve others. Some of the men who were Christians, such as Errol, were so busy in the church that they found it difficult to find time for other things.

> we have a very busy church life, so both of us, my wife and myself, are totally immersed in it, so last year, having a little boy has added a new dimension to life for us, but me in particular. Talking about men and spirituality, I've seen a different part of my life, having a child. Plus being married has helped me, because before I was totally focused on church, career, helping people, so I had no time for myself.

For others church provided a place where they could be themselves Simon talked about the church being a group of like-
minded people with whom one could quickly establish new
relationships.

> One of the things about being a Christian is, wherever one
> goes, if one goes to a different town or city, hopefully one can
> always meet other Christians in a church context and one,
> hopefully, should always be accepted fairly readily. And that
> has always been our experience of moving.

Tony, who is retired, saw his spiritual requirements as 'fairly
simple'. He found it difficult to understand all the 'beating of the
breast' and 'angst' that some people in his church went through.
His own confirmation (in his forties) coincided with his father's
death and was partly influenced by that. For him it is the physical
act of communion which is important.

> It's more than a physical act to me; every time I do it, I have
> something rather more than a physical experience. It's the
> physical act of taking a crust of bread and a sip of wine, but I
> do, with my limited theological knowledge, accept it totally
> and utterly as to what it's supposed to be representing . . . I
> just totally and utterly believe that Jesus Christ was who he
> was . . . the resurrection is what makes Christianity for me.

Although he is a member of a church and a Christian, there are
some aspects of sections of the Church Tony doesn't like:

> The evangelical thing where it's sometimes expressed in
> people wanting to, as it were, apprise others of their situation,
> or convert or whatever it might be – in my opinion, the only
> way that you will ever influence anyone else is by your
> example. If that person sees you, or vice versa, and you want
> something of what that person's got, then you go for it. But I

wouldn't want that person attempting to convert me or bombard me in any way, shape or form, and I wouldn't dream, I couldn't dream of bombarding anybody else with my beliefs. But if somebody else, as a result, feels they'd like to find out a little bit more because they think, 'He's got something that I'd like', that's just great. That's all.

Several talked of their experience of becoming a Christian. Jim became a Christian in his teens and has lived out his faith within the church.

When I was about fifteen, I had a friend that went to the local church youth club and he invited me along. I was going along for quite a few weeks and then one night they had a fifteen-minute epilogue spot, which was quite strange really because I always thought that an epilogue came at the end . . . This one night, I was trying to mind my own business and this girl was talking about the difference that Christ had made in her life. I suddenly realised that she seemed to have something I hadn't. So I made enquiries from there and started to grow in the Christian faith and gave my life to Christ. It wasn't, I suppose, a Damascus road conversion. The little thing where I started listening was the memorable thing about it. I've grown in the faith since then.

For Paul becoming a Christian was a gradual process within the structure of the Anglican Church although there were key rites of passage outside it.

Just after I'd been confirmed, I went with a friend over to a Pentecostal church . . . and there was a youth evangelist there. I remember him saying, 'If you want Jesus to be your Saviour, put up your hand', or some such words. And for me it wasn't a decision, but putting up my hand was a statement of an on-going thing that I wanted, if you know what I mean.

Later on in his life he went to a meeting at college,

> Then I went along to a meeting and somebody said, 'Have
> you ever asked Jesus into your life?' That was the question
> they asked and I didn't hear anything more because it set me
> thinking. 'Now I haven't asked that, but that isn't what I need
> to ask. I know that that isn't the question that I need to ask.
> But maybe I do need to take a step of commitment which
> I've not taken, but I haven't a clue what it is.'
>
> I remember praying the prayer there and then that if there
> was some step of commitment that I need to take, that I could
> take it. And to this day I don't know what that was all about,
> except that what I do know is that after that point, all these
> choruses and peculiar goings-on in prayer meetings, made
> sense. I don't know what happened, but something did and to
> me that was quite important, because it was from that point
> that I can say that I got more involved.

Nick had an experience of God after his wife, who had been ill
for years, suddenly became better – something which he and his
wife saw as divine healing.

> I'd questioned God, you see, over this period of time and said,
> 'Well, if you're a God, why suffering? Why this and why that?'
> I think we all ask those questions some time in life. By this
> time I was about 48 and I'd had odd experiences of God. I
> believe we were brought together by God. And I said, 'If this
> is what God is really like, I want to know him.'
>
> And I went to the church where we lived. I went to
> confirmation classes and all the vicar did was read Luke's
> Gospel and halfway through I realised: I looked up at the
> window, at this Christ up in the window and thought, 'It's
> what you did for me, not what I do for you', because I used
> to think, at that stage, it's what I do for other people that
> counts, what I do for God doing for other people, that counts.

I realised that was really only a part and my whole thinking changed right round at that stage. So that was a very significant change that's made my life completely different from then onwards. For the last fifteen years it's been a life crammed with incidents, with happiness, with sadness, but seeing them as the whole of life, not just individual incidents: part of bringing you to something.

Are Men as Religious as Women?

It is a 'well-known fact' that men are not interested in religion having given it up as a 'woman thing'. Men talk cars, not cassocks. Jeremy Clarkson, the sardonic wit most associated with presenting car programmes on the BBC, probably gets more hero points in the lives of British men than Jesus Christ. A cursory look at the statistics confirms that, compared with women, men are not as strong in their religious belief.[4] A British Social Attitudes Survey confirms this:

- The total believing in God was 48 per cent for men and 70 per cent for women.
- The total believing in a higher power was 15 per cent for men and 11 per cent for women.
- The total not believing was 37 per cent for men and 19 per cent for women.

Two-thirds of the change in church going in the eighties could be accounted for by a fall-off by men.[5]

By any measurement women are more religious than men and their approach to religion is different to men. Men may be in the majority in the pulpits but women are in the majority in the congregation.[6] Errol confirmed this for his own Pentecostal tradition:

... there are a lot more women than men: seven to one or even eight to one ... but men in control. And I think, I've got a vision, I want a vision that we get men back in the Church. We get men back in the Church because we want to get some families and hopefully some family values back.

This difference between men and women is not only true of church attendance but persists throughout all measures of belief and practice. One of the areas where it is most marked is the dimension of private prayer. The Church is often accused of being patriarchal and being one of the institutions that offer women least equality. But if so, why do so many women attend? One of the issues is that as people live longer, more women survive for longer than men so in the elderly population there are more women than men attending church.

In terms of religious belief it is worth recording the difference between men and women in a table (if you don't like tables jump to the next bit!):

Gender Differences in Religious Belief – Britain (%)[7]

	Females	Males
Believe in God	84	67
Do not believe in God	9	16
Believe in sin	72	66
Believe in a soul	76	58
Believe in heaven	69	50
Believe in life after death	57	39
Believe in devil	42	32
Believe in hell	35	27

Perhaps men are most interested in religion when it is publicly expressed rather than privately. Women may feel the opposite. In a world of relationships and private devotion women are freer than in public where men still predominate. Islam and Judaism both attract more men than women and these two religions are still rooted in public life. In the West, religion has become a private optional activity. Sociologist Grace Davie distinguishes between *believers* and *belongers*. In other words our beliefs are not mirrored in our church attendance. The difference between men and women's beliefs is biggest in private devotion, prayer and Bible reading. So female believers may outnumber male believers even more than female belongers outnumber male belongers.[8]

If private faith is becoming more important, then the passing on of religious belief and practice may have to rely on women. But men and women tend to see God in different ways so what is passed on may begin to change if women are the only ones available to do it.[9]

For women, if they are asked to describe the God in whom they believe, concentrate rather more on the God of love, comfort and forgiveness than on the God of power, planning and control. Men, it seems, do the reverse.[10]

Men and women need each other to challenge and support the other's view of God. To challenge: because if women or men restrict themselves to their own natural preferences they will have a distorted view of God. To support: because the other gender's view of God is essential to my own. We each contribute to the other's wholeness.

If men attribute only masculine characteristics to God then the authority they give God will in turn further distort them as men, until it becomes a self-fulfilling prophecy. They look for a masculine God, see him in the pages of the Bible and imitate those values which then reinforce the next round of the same process. Jesus was a man but he did not behave like a typical man. He challenged the masculinity of his culture not by rebelling against the conventions of his day but by honouring women and children and by being a servant to others, such as when he washed his disciples' feet.

But Jesus is not just the God of love and forgiveness. He is also the one who turns over the tables of the money-changers exploiting the poor in the temple, and the one who judges the world. If those of us who want our dodgy behaviour endorsed by God say that he is a God of love and therefore accepts what we are doing we are making a God according to our own preferences. God is also a God of utter purity, a burning Holy Fire. This is a mystery and a paradox but men and women need each other to even come near to understanding it. If men follow a conventionally masculine Christ they worship a distorted God.

If men project onto God the masculine characteristics which have resulted in them living a distorted human life, the end result is a God who only confirms this distortion in their own lives. If the rest of God's character is described in characteristics and actions which men reject because they are traditionally associated with women then it is no wonder that men are in spiritual difficulty.

If God is there to confirm the world view of men then they become more deeply alienated from human wholeness. If God is there to challenge the world view of men then they have to let go of the old world view in order to embrace human wholeness. The same is of course true of women but until recently the Church has suppressed any movement they wished to make in that direction.

The Rise of Fundamentalism

It is important to get definitions right when talking about fundamentalism. There are Christians who are fundamentalists in the sense that they have a strong commitment to the infalli-bility of the Bible and have a tendency to read it literally. Fundamentalism in that sense is not what I am talking about here. Those Christians are part of mainstream Christianity. But there is a rising tide of another form of Fundamentalism (with a capital 'F') which arises from the most explosive mix of masculinity and religion. The rise of Fundamentalism throughout the world in Islam, Judaism and Christianity is a reaction against a perceived threat from the fall in Western moral standards and the need to reassert social and religious values. Fundamentalism is a heady mix of a conviction in the rightness of one's own beliefs, a refusal to dialogue with those who disagree and, in the worst cases, a belief in the essential evil of anybody who disagrees. This position is a defence against a perceived undermining of religious or moral standards.

I mention this because it is especially attractive to men. It puts them in control of others in a way which cannot be questioned since any disagreement can be countered by appealing to the scriptures of that religion. This is quite the opposite to the approach of a Church confidently preaching a message which it is prepared to defend but which is open to question.

The great fear of many social thinkers is that in the twenty-first century there may be a kickback against the mix of freedom, permissiveness and uncertainty which has characterised the end of the twentieth century. There certainly needs to be a return to a commitment to the moral and spiritual life from which we have so disastrously detached ourselves. But Fundamentalism takes away freedom of speech and imposes its views with verbal or physical force. It subjugates women as it always, without fail, re-establishes the authority of men over women in society and family. This potential danger, which seems so far away from us in our culture, means that men must know themselves well and develop a spirituality which is based on love, worship and justice rather than on power and control.

But as we have seen from the work of Grace Davie and Tony Walter, men tend to think of God as a God of power, planning and control. We need to recover the rest of God if we are to recover the rest of ourselves. Think of the list of the elements which should characterise the Christian. The fruit of the Spirit (the Christ-likeness towards which all Christians want to grow) is characterised by: 'love, joy, peace, patience, kindness, goodness, faithfulness, gentleness, self-control. Against such things there is no law.'[11]

This is vital because one of the most frightening aspects of fundamentalism is its attraction to violence. In the case of religious fundamentalism this is a potent mix when placed against the capacity of men to use violence in what is seen as a just cause. Whether the tools used are hit lists published on the Internet containing the addresses of suspected abortionists, or the direct use of force, the paradox is that these people use methods explicitly prohibited by their religion to enforce its central tenets. The Second World War showed how cruelly men could behave in what they call a righteous cause. Jürgen Moltmann, the distinguished German theologian, strikes a chilling note when he says, 'thirty years ago we thought that fundamentalism would disappear. Today it looks as if it will determine the future shape of religion'.[12]

How men are shaped by their relationships, the models of masculinity they are given by their fathers, and the commitment to the spiritual life will have a great influence on how capable men are of resisting the destructive in society and celebrating the good. We turn first to the relationship between fathers and sons.

4

Fathers and Sons

The relationship between fathers and sons is a sacred one. Fathers are there to show their sons what the world looks like through a man's eyes. They are there to demonstrate that gentleness and humility are more powerful than aggression and violence. They provide security and protection in boyhood as their sons explore the limits of their masculinity. A son who has been loved, heard and disciplined has the foundations laid for the rest of his life.

In order to flourish as human beings we need unconditional love. If we are denied it we may survive, but we will struggle as we try and come to terms with the conditions placed on us by our parents in our early years. Unconditional love sees a son as a blessing, a person worthy of dignity, care and nurture. Fathers are no less a parent than mothers though their ways may be different. But it is when love is absent or conditional that a son begins to feel that he is in some sense less than who he is meant to be and spends the rest of his life dealing with that.

Fathering is more than fatherhood. Whereas fatherhood describes the man's role as a parent, fathering is the way in which a father forms a relationship with his son. It is about the mix of discipline and nurture, tenderness and toughness, absence and presence. There were few subjects in the interviews that men spoke about more than their relationship with their father. Fathering can wound and destroy or it can build confidence and self-respect. These men spoke of both.

There comes a time, as boys mature, that they need to be

prepared for adulthood. In our culture one of our chief problems is that young men are not initiated into the adult world of men. There is no ritual which tells boys that they are now men and explains to them how men are called to lead their lives. Girls have a very symbolic time when they begin menstruation which carries with it obvious and enriching messages about the transition from being a girl to being a woman. This process is natural but there is no such natural process for boys.

In other cultures one of the key messages given to initiates to manhood is 'life is hard, life is painful'. The time of childhood play is drawing to a close and a new world is opening up in which men must bear responsibility. In many of those rituals young men are wounded in order to symbolise this. In his autobiography Nelson Mandela tells of his own initiation with both its pain and its sense of honour. The rite of circumcision was used to do this and, as it was done, each boy had to call out '*Ndiyindoda!*' ('I am a man!').

> Before I knew it the old man was kneeling before me. I looked directly into his eyes. He was pale, and though the day was cold, his face was shining with perspiration. His hands moved so fast that they seemed to be controlled by an otherworldly force. Without a word, he took my foreskin, pulled it forward, and then with a single motion, brought down his assegai. I felt as if fire was shooting through my veins; the pain was so intense that I buried my head in my chest. Many seconds seemed to pass before I remembered the cry and I recovered and called out, 'Ndiyindoda!' . . . A boy may cry, a man conceals his pain.[1]

At this point Mandela was given a new name and entered into manhood with all the privileges and responsibilities that entailed.

Boys in our culture have no such rite of passage. Some of them try to show they are men by over-identifying with violence or criminal activity at an early age. Others who have loving fathers are fortunate to learn over time what it means without any such ritual. Still others are always insecure about their masculinity, never really feeling accepted in the world of men. Nelson Mandela's wound was the beginning of a journey to wisdom. But our age supports no such distinctive view of the male spiritual journey as we have just seen. Far from fathers handing on something to their sons, the sons of this generation are frustrated by the mute fathers and by their lack of preparation for the adult world.

A Man is a Father

Despite this the men we interviewed want to be fathers, partly because they want to show that fatherhood can be different. They are keen to participate in the new set of relationships into which they will be drawn by having children. They look forward to doing things with their children and to caring for them. Many of the men spoke of their intention to love and care for their children. Those who had young children and were going through disruption of family routines and losing sleep saw themselves as equal partners in parenting with a strong commitment to their children. In the majority of cases, for prospective fathers, it didn't seem to matter what gender their children would be.

Fatherhood gives men a role and purpose in life. Whatever their prospects at work, success educationally or social background, fathering is something at which all men have a chance of excelling. It is when children come along that the role of a provider is enhanced.

Whether or not they already have children, many men regard being a father as their main purpose in life: Luke, Nathan and Jim all commented on this in one way or another.

I suppose the one thing would be that I really like being a

father; I really genuinely love being a father. I suppose I'm a man if I'm a father.

I'm in my mid-twenties, not got a family yet, so I don't have the perspective a father might have. So I'm confused about what it means to be a real man.

I see myself more as a dad these days than a man.

For the men interviewed who were already fathers this was usually near the top of their agendas in terms of their list of priorities. Those with older children enjoyed it even though it had, for some, brought a great deal of pain.

All talked about their own fathers. Many of the men seemed to use the same kind of language when talking about their fathers. This might be because every generation has a myth about what a father should be, to which all others are compared. For many men the myth has not changed since the dawn of time – until recently that is.

There have been times and cultures in which survival was the highest priority. In such worlds men and women worked hard to protect and sustain themselves, provide for their offspring and pass on their genes to the next generation. Boys passed initiation rites which confirmed them as men. A hard life meant that bravery and risk were essential if the community was to live successfully.

In our own generation we can already see the formation of an ideal of a father who is demonstrative and nurturing and who readily gives up time to be with his children. Does the myth exist? The myth of the ideal father is a dangerous thing. If we apply it to the previous generation of fathers we find ourselves disappointed, because no such ideal fathers existed then. If we allow ourselves to be caught in the same trap we will pass on that dissatisfaction from one generation to another and will become victims of it ourselves. In fathering our sons we must not only talk to them and listen to them but we must also be humble with them about the limits of our own ability to father them.

Perhaps it is better to talk about the 'good enough' father rather than perpetrating the myth of the ideal father. This is not because we have low expectations of ourselves, but because we refuse to compare ourselves with an ideal which has never been achieved and never will be achieved. We all make mistakes with our children. One of the results of rapid change in our world is that what was appropriate even thirty years ago can be readily criticised today. So fathers in a previous generation are weighed in the balances and found wanting in terms of contemporary ideas.

Our own ideas will be judged similarly by our sons in the future. This judgment on a previous generation may seem unfair, but if the ideas which dominated the fathering of a previous generation damaged the sons reared at that time then we may find that it is that fathering which has contributed in large part to the struggles and hurts which so many men present today. In terms of our spiritual lives we have not received that unconditional love which we all need in order to flourish. The only person who practises unconditional love towards us is God.[2]

The New Father

David spoke of having 'a big thing' about being a father which involved,

> Being there, having time for the kids and doing things with the kids, understanding them. And then all the issues around how you discipline them and things like that. So for instance, I don't smack . . . so it's about a proper relationship really and treating them as individuals and not objects.

Childbirth is an important defining moment for men. Whether it is something they envy or prefer to view at a distance, it is important. At least Martyn was honest when he said, 'I wouldn't like to be a woman because of the pain of childbirth.' Mark spoke for several men when he said that the one thing that he really liked about being a man was 'experiencing childbirth without having to go through it.' Jim saw this as a negative in that it was a precious experience for his wife in which he couldn't fully share since she carried the baby inside her.

But childbirth can also be a time when men are forgotten and women are in the spotlight. Martyn obviously felt this keenly.

> The baby's born, all the relatives come round, suddenly you're a cipher. Nobody gives a damn, but you're still expected to bring in the money, to get up, go to work, come back, look after the child.

But for some, such as John and his wife who had a stillborn child, childbirth was a time not for joy but for one of the greatest tragedies of their lives. Others cannot have children and feel a lack of purpose as they look at the future.

Those men who were at the birth of their children found it an unforgettable experience, and several chose this experience as the most exhilarating or memorable moment in their lives. Chris said that for him newborn babies are special because they are like a 'blank page'. 'It's a purity thing in some ways: he's not tainted by the world as yet.'

Edward was present at the birth of both his children and found it even more exhilarating than getting married.

> . . . it's indescribable, I can't describe it. That's what it is even now. Yes it's really made me soft . . . it's such a wonderful thing.

Because Errol's wife's first pregnancy ended with a miscarriage there was concern when she became pregnant for a second time. Errol was at the hospital for the twelve hours she was in labour for their second child, taking part in the birth.

I went to all the sit-down-on-the-cushions classes and whatever, for new fathers, and I enjoyed all that. But the experience of the birth, I must admit, I cried . . . After he made his first cry (because he came out a different way round), I think that broke me then. It will always stay with me, even if I have a second child, I think I will always remember the first. I felt relieved, there were a lot of emotions . . . Joyous in a way. Yes, it was a very joyous occasion. My wife cried. We were a family now and we thanked God because my wife had struggled a lot because of the miscarriage. So it was a mixture of elation, thanksgiving, we cried, we prayed.

Most of the fathers who were divorced placed their children first on their list of the things they looked forward to in their week. This was true whether the children were now grown up or whether they were small. It was also the case even if seeing the children was painful or led to a period of depression after they had left.

All those men who wanted to be fathers or who had young children used the language of love and nurture to describe their relationship with their children. As well as playing with them and enjoying them they also expected to talk with them and be the fathers to their children that many of them never had. Yet later in the interviews these men also talked about the difficulties they had in expressing their emotions. How do these two things square up? One interviewee recalled an incident when he and his father were looking over the crib where his new baby son was sleeping. He was a man who had experienced difficulties with his father who could be silent and unemotional. He talked about how he wanted to make time for his son, to love him and to be able to share his life with him. 'Yes,' his father said, 'that's what I said when you were born.'

The Silent Father

Both father and son find themselves in difficulties when the strengths of one generation are weaknesses for the other. A man may have had a hard life and steeled himself to work, fight and provide in the most difficult circumstances. In doing that he has suffered, not least by refusing to listen to his emotions. He may be a man who visits his son and shows his care by doing DIY jobs around the house. He may be proud of what his children have accomplished but does not understand their world. Relating to him is cross-cultural communication and a perfect example of 'it's not what you say that matters, it's what they hear'.

I tried to have a conversation with my father about two years ago to tell him how I felt, because that was one of my big areas of difficulty, that I didn't really get on with my father, never had done. I tried to do that, really, really, really hard, over a period of about three months. I didn't just slap him round the face with it saying. 'This is what we're going to do'. I couldn't get through to him at all. That's something I very much regret. Even to this day I'm still trying to do it, but not so aggressively as I was.

But during some of those confrontations – confrontations? – conversations, I gave some examples of things that had happened in the past and how they had made me feel and tried to get him to talk about how he had felt, and he just totally refused to participate. I felt that it was my own fault, because I was stupid or whatever. He wasn't prepared to express his feelings. At the time it annoyed me but what I can see now is I got to where I am because I wanted to find out about myself, really, and my father has decided what he is and how he is and he's not going to change. He's one of the stiff upper lip brigade and all that. And I don't knock him for that but I still do find it quite frustrating.

That sense of frustration is not confined to an aggressive and frustrated son trying to prise open a father characterised as 'stiff upper lip'. Patrick's father has a different personality but the same response. He starts by talking positively about his father and then mentions that he is probably a disappointment to his father. He doesn't *know* if he is. He just thinks he might have been.

> A sweet man, a kind man. He won't die, he'll fade away. Both my parents are still alive. He has no special interests. A man. But actually he had very little impact on me. He wanted me to be sporty and outgoing and I was introspective and un-sporty, so that will be a disappointment to him. I think he and I remain incomprehensible to each other, although we get on okay. We've always got on okay because there's nowhere that we meet. We meet physically in rooms and I see quite a lot of them and they go on holiday with us, but our minds never meet and our feelings never meet . . . It's sad but I don't know what he thinks of me.
>
> Well, I talk to a lot of people whose parents are very close to them and actually mine aren't and the awful thing is, I think, that when they die, I don't think I will be very upset. In fact, I don't think it will make any difference to me at all and that is a shocking, deeply shocking thing for me to say out loud, but it's what I think.

Here is a father who is 'kind' and 'gentle', both characteristics we might associate with the modern idea of the new man. But the relationship between father and son is just not there. Did they not talk to one another? Perhaps he's right. He was a disappointment to his father and it is that burden which he carries around now.

Nick's father wasn't prepared to talk to him even when he had an obligation as a parent to do so. He didn't seem to be able to talk personally. He didn't know the language. Maybe when he looked for it he found that it wasn't there. As a very young teenager Nick was vulnerable. First, it needed courage to go to his father. Second, it was an act of trust to admit his ignorance. His father neither recognised nor responded to either of these things:

> My father is sociable and enjoys going out with people, but we've never talked about anything that might be considered personal. We never talked about sex or what you were supposed to do. We say hello and we have a bit of a chat about how it's going and the rest of it, but it doesn't really move on any further than that, which I suppose is a shame. When I was young, I sat there one night and I thought, 'Well he hasn't mentioned it so I'll ask him about this sex thing: What are we supposed to do?' But he didn't answer the question; it just died a death. I think I must have been about thirteen or fourteen when I asked. I find it difficult . . . In my own mind I just think it's pointless. We didn't speak about these things when we were younger. I can't imagine for the life of me we're going to do it now. Heaven forbid that he's going to be on his deathbed and blub all this out in an emotional two-hour chunk!

The Unemotional Father

Fathers and sons who do not understand one another will also have a relationship which is emotionally strained. But fathers are called to love their children and to live in a way which models the kind of life they want their children to live. Perhaps the fathers of a previous generation thought they were doing that. Perhaps they just got it wrong.

It is remarkable that so many of these men still respect their fathers despite the way they have behaved. This doesn't mean that they want to copy their father. Perhaps men make the mistake of regarding closeness as a childish quality they need to abandon as adults. Ironically, the opposite is true: to be mature they need to develop more adult forms of closeness.[3] Nathan commented,

> I hope I will have children and that I'll be the father that my dad wasn't. My dad is a great person and everything – he and my mum are still together and I was never abused or anything as a child, but my dad didn't show emotion. I hope that I'll show emotion with my kids and I hope that I'll take them to football matches . . . which never happened to me, and that's maybe why I hate sports.
>
> My relationship with my father now is an intellectual relationship. He goes on and on about things to the nth degree. We only see my mum and dad probably once every three or four months. When we get together, the conversation is always round my dad and me, really, and Rosy more recently, because she realised it's the only way to say anything. My dad's hung up on things like genetics and how that affects people's behaviour. Me being a trendy, bleeding heart liberal will say, 'No, it's society.' We rehearse the same argument every time we meet up and it's all up here, it's all in the head. When I hug him at the end of the weekend and say goodbye, we do it, but it feels strange, forced a bit, really. We do this thing where we shake hands and hug at the same time. For the last year I realised that it is really strange, but our arms are held together in this barrier between us. We don't hug like . . . full-bodied. There's a distinct lack of emotion.

Asked whether his father would be surprised to hear him say this he said,

> I don't know, that's the sad answer.

Andy converted to Christianity a few years ago. He is stepfather to two boys he has raised since they were babies and is also a grandfather. Although he has a part-time job he is not in good health. As a child he had his share of playing truant and stealing, and spent time in a children's home and then borstal. But he remembers a happy childhood.

Although Andy loved his dad it did not mean that his father's influence was always healthy. Destructive patterns of behaviour can also be handed on. For Andy it was drinking heavily:

I started drinking early. My dad, he drank, but he was a good man. He was a good man, really. Ours was a big family; a lot for him to put up with when he came home. So he'd be out to the pub. In the area where we lived everybody drank. That was the type of upbringing that we had. I worship my dad, always did. I can remember my dad, when I was young, he used to take me fishing, he used to take me to his grandparents. He was a very fit man because I can remember him carrying me on his shoulders.

But it wasn't an emotional relationship. It wasn't really. There was none of that there. You couldn't really show it. I think it was just something I knew and something he knew. The same with mother. You couldn't put your arms round her. I think that's mainly my dad's background. His family was all whisky drinkers. Strict, strict, very disciplined people.

Later on he said, 'the closest person I ever had to talk to was my dad'.

The Absent Father

Silence or lack of emotion is a wounding experience but some wounds go even deeper. Luke survived his experience of his father's rejection but didn't emerge unscathed.

My parents never got on. My mum wasn't happy in the marriage in the days when it was harder to get out. So it was not a happy household. She tended to take it out on my dad and other people around her. He was a fairly compliant, passive character who would basically sit and take it, so it took the form of nagging but I think it was more about her expressing her unhappiness with no obvious result.

The culmination of that was that when I was about thirteen they separated and my dad went to work abroad. Shortly after all that happened, she became ill with cancer for the next eighteen months and died when I was fifteen and a half. My dad came back and nursed her through her last illness. Once she had died he went back abroad again and I went into lodgings. He supported me financially. I was still at school. So from fifteen to about nineteen, when I went to university, it was emotionally very, very hard.

I spent many years in my teens being very angry with my dad. He didn't visit me very often and was more happy to write a cheque. He's dead now but I think I realised before he died, that I was saying, 'You've left me and I just want you to come back and look after me.' But I couldn't say it in words, because it would have gone against me surviving and looking up. I was OK . . . getting by and things. But it was a very numb, denied time, more than anything else . . . But the other side of what happened was that none of the extended family, none of them offered to look after me, and I think another element of my anger was the fact that I felt quite abandoned by them as well. I realised again in recent years how angry I was about that.

Afterwards Luke put everything emotional on hold:

I feel in retrospect that had I let it come out, I would have been overwhelmed, and had I not had that religious time, I think I would have probably gone into a situation of – I don't know – drinking heavily or drugs or something. I think I would have done something fairly negative with it all.

Luke had an intense period of Christian activity and teaching while at college but then 'went away from it'. He is now continuing his search through counselling which is the 'most spiritual thing that has happened in recent years'.

The Caring Father

These bad and hurtful experiences of fathers have to be put in the context of several men who had caring fathers who loved them and whom they loved in return. Dan is one man who knew his father loved him as a child but didn't have a chance to talk to him until recently.

My father is very caring, he's very loving and he also wants to provide. He wants to make sure that we can provide for ourselves and be secure financially. I think some of that is due to his background, because his father died when he was a child and there was no will or anything so there was no security. So that's something very much on my father's heart.

Saying that, there's been changes in my father which have been really good to see. I think I missed out on a lot with him. That's something which I want to rectify. And we're starting to, so that's good. We are having weekends when it's just us, able to go off, maybe walking, cycling or whatever it is, where we can just be and share and talk. He can say how things are going in his work and I have the opportunity to say how I am, how I feel. We can catch up on – not time lost – but time that wasn't there.

Some men spoke briefly about how they saw their fathers. Len was one of these,

Very hard working, very conscientious, very supportive and still is, very encouraging . . . We've got closer as we've got older. I had a very secure loving background.

Dennis said that if he were here now his father would be very proud of him and this was mirrored in the way he saw his father and tried to emulate him. Others had grandfathers or elder brothers as well. When asked about his parents Dennis replied.

I think I'm very similar to my father. He was a generous sort of chap, he got on well with everyone and I think I've learned quite a lot from him. I also had somebody else who I worked with . . . and he really was a generous good-hearted bloke. The things he did, the things that you didn't really hear about, that he was doing to help people. Really impressed me and stuck with me. I just try to emulate these people.

Michael and his father spent time in each other's company and though they were not particularly close when Michael was a child, their relationship developed.

My father was always very keen to help me with my home-work. For example, if I was learning verbs he would test me on them to see that I'd learnt them, and went through them until I could reproduce them. Or if I'd done some written work, he would always look through it and see whether I'd made any spelling mistakes and that sort of thing, which I could then correct. He was very keen on helping in those sort of ways.

And then, moving on a step from there, we developed a sort of pattern of activity whereby towards the end of the evening my father and I would go out for a short walk, just before bedtime, as a way of settling us both down for the night. We were able to have quite a number of chats, of course, during these evening walks. So I felt that I got to know my father a lot better, just over that last year or two of school.

Then of course again, during the fairly long vacations . . . we took up this pattern of going for walks . . . my father was in fact a very keen walker and he had always taken me for country walks, because my mother had never been a robust walker; she had only gone on short walks.

I think I gradually realised, over my career, that I have a lot of similarity with my father. He, I think, was a very meticulous person, that's what helped him, I think, to progress so well in his career. I've realised that I'm a meticulous sort of person, always wanting to make sure that whatever I do, I do it properly and get it right.

I can't just pinpoint other characteristics, but I keep being aware of characteristics in myself which I know are similar to characteristics that I know I've remembered in my father, although as I say the other characteristics I can recognise from my mother too, especially this sort of reticence and slight inferiority complex, you might call it, of not expecting to do well or being apprehensive that I might not be able to cope.

In this chapter on fathers there seems at first glance to be a lot of ambiguity. Men might know that their fathers loved them and respected them but feel that they didn't get what they wanted out of the relationship. Perhaps this was due to three things.

First, the men of this generation are living in a new world and so in many cases this discontinuity has meant that sons feel that they have to set out on their own without the support of their fathers' experience and wisdom.

This is the cross-over generation in which the model of the traditional father competes with other alternatives. For generations to come this change will be of historical interest (unless of course we move back to the traditional model) but for the current generation it is an emotional and psychological inheritance. This is why there is so much reflection on it at the moment and why so many men are processing it. Of course in the future there will still be fathers and sons who have good or bad relationships but this cross-over period is particularly important socially.

Second, many sons felt emotionally estranged from their fathers. Understanding that their fathers lived in a different world didn't help sons who had directly appealed to their fathers for help and had been turned down, even at a very young age, to build good relationships with them. Many of the fathers used non-verbal intimacy to express their care, and while this is sometimes very effective, it is not an appropriate response when a son is asking a question. Even if the father found emotions difficult to handle he could have said *something*.

This raises the importance of forgiveness between fathers and sons together with the need for reconciliation. Sons who harbour hurt and resentment against their fathers need to forgive them. But so do fathers! If the father's attitude towards his son is due to something he has done in the past or disappointment with him, then, in order for the relationship between them to prosper, the father needs to forgive him.

Third, looking at the interviews as a whole, one of the aspects which is missing can be summed up in the biblical practice of blessing. In the Old Testament particularly, fathers would bless their sons. Sometimes a father would do this before death as an act of passing on responsibility to the eldest son. But the idea of blessing somebody was widespread throughout Jewish culture. In doing so fathers would signify not only that they wanted their sons to have a fruitful and prosperous life but also that they approved of them.

Many of the sons interviewed here did not want a life of emotion with their fathers although they would have liked a father who would talk to them. After all without conversation no relationship can change. They would have liked to have been blessed by their father. They would have liked to have received their father's approval, to know that their father thought they had turned out OK. A lot has been written about the importance of boys being initiated into manhood but little, if anything, has been written about the need for fathers to bless their sons, releasing them from the anxiety or uncertainty about their opinion of them and lovingly conveying their desire that they might prosper in what they are doing.

The idea of initiation ceremonies coming back is less likely than the possibility that fathers may renew their commitment to blessing their sons. However, blessing is a prayer. Its power lies in asking God to bless the son in the future. A blessing involves two fathers.

5

Men and Women

Communities are built on the partnerships between men and women. Without commitment between them there is no future for us. It is here that the rate of change in culture and the pressures that have resulted from it are felt most keenly. Everybody knows about the irresponsibility of the modern man, his unfaithfulness or lack of loyalty.

When men and women separate, we are told that men have to be chased by government agencies to make maintenance payments. Who is responsible for the increasing number of single parent families? By default it is assumed that it must be men since it is mostly women who are left bringing up the family. Divorce affects one in three marriages. There is a lot of pain out there. Fewer children are being brought up in families by both natural parents.

The relationship between men and women is changing in other ways too. Research from Stanford University in the US tells us that 50 per cent of men feel uncomfortable in the presence of women and that flirting is dying a death because of men's fear of sexual harassment allegations. Jokes are told and adverts used about men which are sexist and, if aimed at women, would be accused of being discriminatory or of causing offence. All is not well between men and women.

Traditionally marriage is a covenant between two people before God in the presence of the community. It is intended to be public, permanent and monogamous. It is based on powerful promises made by one person to another 'until death us do part'. This is serious stuff. It is not about 'until love disappears' or 'until I realise I have married the wrong person'. Yet marriages go wrong. They can end up causing such pain that people live in agony. They can be the context in which adultery and deceit seem to flourish. Divorce can quickly appear to be the only way of resolving marital difficulties, and the easier it is to obtain it, the more acceptable it becomes (or is it the other way round?). Marriage is giving way to cohabitation even though the average cohabitation lasts only two years, and a woman has very few rights compared to somebody who is married.

Domestic violence and abuse add to the problem. In such cases women and children need to be rescued, protected and offered the due process of law. Here again it is men who, however incited, are nearly always responsible for violence although the phenomenon of 'battered husbands' is now surfacing as a hidden but serious problem. It seems that this latter issue has remained hidden because of the shame men go through when it happens, their unwillingness to 'hit back' because of their superior strength and the fear of what it would do to their partner, as well as the feeling abused men have that the law would be on the side of the woman.

But Michael, viewing the general scene from near retirement, felt that things have come a long way:

I think society has moved to a very good position at the moment, where there is much more of this feeling of equality and yet the little extra bits of things that men do and women appreciate still happen and are still appreciated.

He didn't make any comments about the little bits that aren't appreciated.

Frank found it difficult to reconcile his views on spirituality and religion with the difficulties he and his wife were facing,

I have a fairly traditional attitude to spirituality, in the sense that we are part of – I was going to say a family – an organisation, a movement, a family, that should accept and live by standards of tolerance, of compassion, and a sense of right and wrong. I can see that in the sense of our marriage in this present time. We have talked about this and started going for counselling. My view is that I took a vow, which is a vow based upon this belief that it is for life, for good and bad and all the rest of it, in sickness or in health. That's very important to me and so I do not accept, really, the principles of divorce, but I am beginning to get to the view that if the incompatibility is so basically strong, that people can make mistakes and the biggest mistake of all is to continue to cause each other pain and anger. So I'm finding that a very difficult process to go through, which I haven't solved.

Forgiveness is not the same as pardon. It does not mean pretending that something never happened. We have to live with where our memory has been. If somebody has done something wrong then restitution has to be made and forgiveness does not remove the need to go through that process. Forgiveness is about letting go of something. Holding on to a bitter past means we are trapped. A guilty person needs to be forgiven. A wronged person needs to forgive. The initiative can start from either side and does not depend on whether a person is guilty or wronged. But sometimes the situation can be painful as Martyn illustrated in the case of someone he loved.

Unfortunately she married the wrong bloke . . . it was the stress of it all, really, which killed her, I think. I still blame him for that, I really do. If I never see him again it will be too soon . . . I don't like violence anyway and to see the aftermath of a violent attack on someone you love is incredibly distressing. But it was her choice. She had a chance to leave him but she loved him so much that she wouldn't. And I feel at a loss, really, for that.

In our day, when relationships are negotiated rather than assumed, this focus on love and respect is at the heart of human relationships and is essential in marriage. It is the abuse of this mutuality which lies at the heart of so much pain.

A Loving Relationship

How do men talk about those they love? Andy talked about how he looked forward to the weekend when he could spend time with his wife. He really admired her marvellous ability to mix socially.

> I just love being with her. I love my wife a lot, I think the world of her. It's been difficult with us. Not a difficult marriage but hard – especially with the youngest lad – it's never been easy. A lot of problems. All through that time my wife has always been very, very busy at work, but through it (we've been married twenty years) I've never changed towards her. I still think the world of her, still love her a lot, and I just love being with her. We love to go on holiday together, we love to go out together, we love to do everything together . . . I just treasure the times together, really. I care for her more and more, as well, since I got older.

Several men said that they found it easier to confide in women than in men although as we shall see this has its problems. Richard spoke of having close female friends:

> I've got two or three. Funnily enough they're all mature ladies; they're all probably over fifty. I don't see so much of them now as I used to. Going back two or three years ago when I

first split up, I was lost, really, because I had all this time on my hands and nothing to do with it and I was feeling pretty low and down. I just bumped into one of those one day and she started, 'Well come round and have dinner one night', and I did. She helped me a lot and once she started I thought, 'Perhaps I ought to look up these other women, because I haven't really spoken to them much and they all supported me in different ways. It was quite easy – well I say 'easy'; it's not easy – but there was no like (what's the word? Not threat), there was no chance we were ever going to have any sort of relationship other than be friends, because neither of us were looking for that from one another, so it was quite comfortable being in that situation. For them and for me, I think.

The reason most men gave for this kind of relationship was that women brought something different to a friendship that couldn't be found with men, namely they discussed feelings and were prepared to listen to a man who was struggling with a particular situation. But on the other hand some of the men saw no difference between their male and female friends.

Michael appreciated female friends not only because of the impact of them on him,

I was very keen on having lots of girlfriends when I was at university, and in the days immediately before and after that. And I very much value, in fact all the friendships I've had with women in those days. I haven't had close relationships with women, obviously, since getting married. Married life has been very happy for me and I've been very happy with the female companionship I've had from my wife and again with my sister and the wives [of my friends] or my wife's brothers and that sort of thing.

So I feel I've had quite a fair share of female companionship as well, and very much value it because, again, I enjoy the feminine approach to life, the more caring, gentler perhaps more artistic, more broad-sweeping approach that women have to life, more than most men have. I think, in a sense, that coincides with the gentler, more caring side of my own personality, which then finds expression more easily with female companionship than it does with male companionship.

The Right Motives?

Some relationships can be founded on the wrong (if sincere) motives. It can be very easy to tell somebody who is about to enter a relationship that it is doomed from the outset, but sometimes they cannot take advice because they feel compelled by some other motive. In Mark's case it was a mistaken sense of responsibility for a girlfriend.

Mark heard that his ex-girlfriend was ill with mental health problems. He contacted her again, feeling in some way responsible, and persuaded himself that he did want to go out with her again. Then he asked her to move in with him again. But when she did she was extremely ill. He became stressed and the relationship broke down. Looking back on that time, several years later, from the vantage point of a happy relationship with someone else, he can see that he shouldn't have done what he did, against the advice of friends. He did it for the wrong reasons. He either felt responsible for her since they had split up, or it could have been an attempt to solve his own loneliness at that time. Either way, it was no basis for a relationship.

Betrayal

When the men interviewed told stories about divorce rather than mentioning it in passing it was because they were in pain and needed to talk about it. In this section we look at three stories about divorce told by Martyn, Alan and Barry.

Martyn's wife was in a serious accident and he did all the housework for several years. Two years into that period they had another baby and there seemed to be light at the end of the tunnel, but soon after that his wife went off with someone else. He felt betrayed. He had worked himself to a 'frazzle', nursing her and caring for the children. Then she got bored with him and went off with somebody else. Now his ex-wife has remarried and the children call her husband 'daddy' which distresses Martyn. His ex-wife also changed his daughter's name.

> Somebody else got the benefit of it. It's like going to the Olympics and coming second. You want to win the big race but on the last track someone overtakes you and gets the gold.

If men who have few if any close male friends then find the one person they have invested all their trust in, betrays that trust, where are they to go?

Continuing Conflict

Richard and his wife are separated. Although they went to marriage guidance, they weren't able to work out their difficulties. Now the high point of Richard's week is seeing his children although he does have other things he looks forward to. If there is a theme in Richard's story it is that although conflict may lead to separation or divorce, it doesn't mean that it won't continue or even get worse. Other relationships may get drawn into it.

Richard usually sees his children once a week for up to three hours and has his children round for tea once a week although, in addition, he does talk to them on the phone. Towards the end of his time with them he becomes melancholic about not spending as much time with them as he would like. He feels low for two or three hours afterwards. His girlfriend, Linda, caused a lot of resentment in the family because her coming closed the door on the possibility of him and his wife getting back together. Now the children will not come round if they think that Linda is going to be there.

He doesn't know what to do because he is planning to live with Linda near his ex-wife and children. Their opposition to this possibility is causing him a great deal of distress. Yet he does feel close to his children because he took an active part in parenting (changing nappies etc.) and has tried to be honest with them about his faults. But this is a monologue. They never talk to him about what they are feeling, preferring to talk to their mother. The divorce is coming up and he worries about the financial pressures it will bring since he is in a lot of debt. Besides Linda he has nobody else to whom he can talk. Although he sees a friend occasionally they're not 'closely involved with each other's lives'. His other friendship with his best man, Dave, has been reduced to Christmas cards.

Legal Battles

Barry was having a struggle getting through each day because of the stress he was under. His ex-wife had just started another legal process with regard to the children so solicitor's letters were coming through the door. The battle over their children had been going on for years. He copes by having a drink and going to the football. He loves football and enjoys going to see Forest. His wife ran off with someone else. It changed his life and he experienced discrimination at first hand.

The first time I took the boys, we went off to Crete and it was a single parent's holiday, which had a special discount . . . Everybody's assumption was that I was a separated dad who was taking the kids off. I found that offensive and hurtful . . . I wouldn't walk out on the kids.

Barry said that he was hit very hard by what happened and lost his confidence. His wife was having an affair with a man from work. He confronted her and she eventually admitted it. The aspect that hit him hardest was the possibility that he might lose the children.

> For a few days, three or four days, . . . I didn't venture out of the house. Stayed in with the kids and cried a lot. Very difficult to get out and face . . . This one couple I went to see and another friend phoned up and I went to see him with the kids. Went back to work – I was off about five days which isn't very long.

Barry sees himself as a father. He is dedicated to the children and does a lot with them, getting up at six o'clock in the morning and coming home to help with cooking and putting them to bed. He's aware that he blends in at the pub, but that although people may know about his views on football, they know nothing about how much he has to do to get to the pub, nor the stress he is going through. He sees close friends as important,

> People that you can enjoy, in the respect that you can do things for them, they do things for you, you can just talk. People that you trust with everything about yourself and your kids and everything.

Len's wife left him just before Christmas. Although he was expecting it he felt,

> . . . absolutely gutted. In fact it was really horrible around Christmas time. My . . . daughter was superb, getting me through that, because she stayed with me for most of Christmas and, 'Let's get a tree', and 'Help me decorate it'. Whereas if it had just been left to me, I don't think I would have bothered. But she was really good. And January was pretty grim, but I

don't like January anyway, with it being so cold and dark. I sometimes wonder whether if it had happened at this time of year, I would have felt so bad about it, with it being a more pleasant time of the year. I think perhaps I would.

. . . Recently, it's got a bit easier because at least I realised a few weeks ago I'm not walking around on broken glass thinking, 'What ought I to say to make things better? What shouldn't I say to make things worse? What ought I to do? What shouldn't I do?'

. . . I've finally done, I think, what I said I'd do a few weeks or months ago but hadn't done, to say, 'Right God, it's in your hands. I'm going to carry on praying about it, but I'm not going to worry about it. And if there's anything you want me to do about it, you show me please.'

. . . I've got a peace about it that I haven't had before certainly.

A Bit on the Side

One interviewee talked about the need to keep relationships with women at a casual level in case a line was overstepped and difficulties arose. He had experienced this himself. It all started innocently with him talking to a woman who was married about their common faith.

After a while they became seriously involved with one another. He tried to stop it but their relationship got very emotional. There seemed no way to escape, besides the damage had already been done. The affair then came out into the open. He went round to the house several times to try and persuade her to stay with her family. He thought, 'I was a Christian, how could it happen?' They had used Scripture to try and rationalise what they were doing, although it was wrong. They also used the fact that there were problems with the marriage to justify the relationship.

You know when you read about the stories and you pass judgment and you sit there thinking, 'Oh dear, how could they do that? It's disgusting.' And I sit there thinking, 'I'm in it.' They would say the same things. And now I just say, 'If you'd only been there.' . . . I thought about committing suicide. There's no way I would, but the thought was that if I committed it, everything would be all right. But I didn't do that . . . it was quite bad and the thing was that other people saw it.

I was in there, I was lying, I was being secretive, I was deceitful, I was using the Bible to cover up my own gain. Inside, I was still asking God, 'Lord, how do I get out of this?' God says he always provides a way out; that wasn't just for me, that would be for everybody in the situation.

He decided to throw away his faith and 'run from God' but when he went to friends at the church they persuaded him not to do that but to work things through. In talking about what had gone wrong he spoke a great deal about not having been under 'authority'. He felt that many of the problems he had had in his life were because he had refused to put himself under some kind of authority. He had abused the freedom he had been given.

How is it possible to sum up the experiences of these men with women without making some kind of facile conclusion that all relationships are different? One important consideration is perhaps that 75 per cent of all divorces are initiated by women. In the majority of these cases, far from the men going off with other women, it is the women who have left the home. The men concerned have not been unemotional, traditional men who have shrugged off their pain. They have, to use Len's phrase, been 'gutted'.

Second, where relationships with women do not have proper boundaries, men and women can both encounter difficulties. When an inappropriate attraction develops between a man and a woman, delusion and deceit swiftly follow. In the case of the adulterous relationship between the couple who were Christians they even used verses from the Bible to try and justify their relationship. Clear boundaries are important to foster the trust between men and women on which the health of the family and the community depends.

Third, in the past, the authority of the man was imposed on the woman and supported by recourse to Scripture. This is no longer the case. As I mentioned above, relationships in marriage are negotiated. Even in traditional marriages there was a large degree of negotiation about the roles of men and women within marriage. But if men want the respect of their wives they cannot assume it will be given automatically. The only respect a man can have in life is that which is freely offered because of the way he lives his life. The love and respect that all marriages need is now seen as mutual and not one way. That change is welcome. Once again negotiation requires conversation and mutual listening.

But marriage is going through a crisis partly because people do not want to make promises they cannot keep; because promises are seen as creating an oppressive structure rather than freedom; because individuals are disillusioned by their experience of other marriages such as their parents'; or increasingly because society no longer sees cohabitation as a sinful activity. It is difficult to anticipate what the future holds for marriage, but from the experiences of these men it is evident that some men are going through real pain in their relationships with women and they need friends around them to listen to them and support them.

6

Men and Friendship

The basic building block of our identity as human beings is that we are 'persons in relationship'. If we have no relationships with others then we will suffer. It is in the context of relating to others that we discover our own identity. So many of the words which describe what it means to be human are words which assume our interdependence. Words such as love, justice, mercy, forgiveness make no sense if we are without relationships and, in the case of those words, open and committed relationships.

It is against this background that so much concern has been felt over contemporary men. Part of the modern stereotype is that men do not have close friends and find it difficult to be open with those they have, or trust them with things which are important to them. If this is true then not only does it reflect on problems with men's relationships but also with problems they are experiencing personally with their own identity and with their view of themselves.

But are these perceptions correct? We can only find out by listening to men's voices and by hearing what they say about themselves and their relationships. In this chapter we deal with friendships between men.

In an age when many marriages are breaking down, the issue of friendship between men has moved from something which is desirable to something which is urgent. If a man is faced with divorce then, as the stories in this book indicate, he will go through a crisis. If he has looked to his wife for all his support and friendship then suddenly it will all disappear overnight. He will need at least one trusted friend with whom he can share what is going on. In situations of crisis circles of friendship are a great support. Of course this is not a primary reason for making friends but in a divorce culture the absence of friendship means that a higher proportion of men will fall apart.

Friendship is one of the most important ways through which we experience intimacy. There are different levels of intensity and ways of expressing friendship. Perhaps one of the problems in talking about men and friendship is that this diversity has not been given sufficient emphasis. Men are perceived to have a difficulty with opening up to others and this is therefore seen as a problem with friendship. But in talking to men about their friends there was a wide spectrum of responses on the subject.

Chris was pretty blunt about the subject. He didn't have any close male friends, had never had any close male friends and didn't care if he ever had any. But he acknowledged that there might be a good reason for his situation. He had spent his life travelling from one place to another with the army and was always saying goodbye to people. Although he had friends (even 'good' friends) there was nobody to whom he would tell his personal problems, nobody with any 'really deep concern'.

Well a close friend for me would be somebody I could tell absolutely everything to and not think that maybe one day it might come back to haunt me. Because I think men are notoriously bad about dropping their friends in the crap, because I think, to be honest, if you're a man you don't know what an emotional crisis is unless you're having one.

Ben didn't have any close male friends either but he had a high view of friendship itself.

I've got male friends who tend to be husbands of my wife's friends who I get on well with. I have got male friends who

I've met independent of my wife, but they're not close friends, I wouldn't confide in them, because if I want to confide in anybody, I confide in my wife, you see. I don't feel I need to go somewhere and talk to somebody . . . I had a mate at school, who I still keep in touch with, but I've got less in common with him now. If I met him for the first time now, I wouldn't have much to do with him, because he's a bit of a prat.

But for Ben the word 'close' meant 'unconditional' so his expectations of a close friendship with another man were very high. He did say that if he was lonely and needed someone to confide in he didn't know how he would go about it. For him friendship was more difficult for men than women because men were less open and more suspicious whereas women were more open and mutually supportive. Women look after each other whereas men try and deal with issues on their own first. Friendship between men was more about having a shared interest.

. . . men, I suppose, become friendly with each other by having a shared interest, like going somewhere. Say you're a season ticket holder at a football match and you're sitting next to this fellow every week, you strike up a conversation and you get to know each other.

Another way of getting a close friend was to have known somebody from childhood. Len said that he had that kind of friendship. They had known each other since they were at primary school together and even if they didn't see each other for months they were able to pick up the relationship without any problems. Len also had no problem with 'comfortable silence' which he saw as a part of real friendship, 'you're not thinking, "Why isn't he talking?" or "What should I say?" ' As far as he was concerned, friendship between men was fairly easy. However, he found it difficult to share his emotions and this had been especially true when he had been through a period of depression due to the stress of work. This was also a difficult time as his wife had just left him. Expressing anger seemed to be OK for men, but he was very wary of expressing vulnerability and would need to know the person really well before opening up on that level. It was easy to get hurt.

Gordon is now 'out' as a gay man. He was married and had children but is now living with his male partner. Despite his being gay he has several close friends who are either straight or with whom he has no sexual relationship,

I've got at least one, two, three good friends where sex is not an issue: it's actually been brought up and discarded very clearly. It's been opened out as an issue, looked at, packed away, because it's not an issue any longer. That's then allowed the furtherance of a relationship, to the point where the guy who's my best friend has actually told me about his HIV status and what's happening with him at the moment. And it allows me in in a way that I probably couldn't have been with other people: I can actually put my arms round him and hold him. I could do that before I knew his status anyway, but it made him feel safe enough to be able to disclose to me, because he knew where I stood and what that was about. So the friendship's much clearer, I think, much more solid.

You still find yourself open to abuse; you still find yourself thinking you've got a friend and you may disclose information to them and you find that it's being misused. I had that recently with someone who employs my son, who is a friend, or was a friend. May still be a friend; he's not talking to us.

Other men talked of close friendship in terms of gentleness and kindness, seeing it as a two-way process which needed give and take as well as being willing to make sacrifices for the other person. But making friends was not easy; male friendship had its downside, as Errol pointed out:

As I've got older, I tend to be very picky because sometimes with . . . some male friends, it's competition and 'I must do better than you' comes in: 'I must get a better job', 'I must earn more money than you', 'I must drive a better car', 'I must have a bigger house'. These things sometimes intrude.

Meeting somebody at the pub seems to be a regular occurrence. Ahmed met somebody at the pub who was on the same shifts as him and they struck up a friendship but he was unsure about trusting him and thought he might not tell him certain things. If he really wanted to say how he felt he would talk to his mum.

Gordon, whom we met earlier, goes even further in his description of a close friendship. A friend is . . .

Someone who, whilst at the same time doesn't take you for granted, gathers gently and carefully information they can use to support you and maybe challenge you at times, so that they keep you – not entirely on your toes, but at least perhaps grounded, sort of like a nudge in the ribs: 'you're flying too many kites. Come back to earth.' . . . Someone who would actually be there come what may but at the same time would say, 'I can't handle this; you've got to give me space and time to handle what's going on, because I really can't deal with this at the moment.'

But what if you are very shy? How do you make friends then? It may be that the macho man hasn't got 'close friends' only 'mates' but what about the shy man? For Nick this was one of his biggest problems in life. He found having relationships with children easier than relationships with adults. Friendship could only happen in a 'working' situation. In a 'being' situation it was very difficult. He gave a lot to young people through his work at a nearby athletics club but said, 'men have a problem to give themselves, and I have probably as

big a problem as anybody.' Nick took after his father who was
a very shy man and though he had pushed his problem deep
inside him, it was still there. Despite this, he and his wife
told each other everything and he thought he was good at
recognising his own emotions.

What do you do if you don't have many close friends but you
are open and have something you want to discuss? For David
this is a real issue: he has a whole string of people he is friends
with but these friendships are intermittent. So were his friendships close?

> Yes, I would like them to be closer. There are certain things
> that are difficult to talk about – this will sound arrogant – I
> think that I'm quite open and I'm really prepared to have this
> type of conversation with those two for instance (Terry and
> Kenneth). I sometimes feel I get nothing back and I feel
> dissatisfied then. So I have a current issue at the moment that
> I have nobody that I can just have a good honest talk to,
> without feeling either dissatisfied or uncomfortable: does he
> really want to talk about this? So that is a lack at the moment
> . . . There's also a very practical reason . . . my wife doesn't
> play football.

Many men talked about being afraid that others would
interpret intimacy wrongly. On some occasions this meant that
they missed out on affection from other men because of this
fear. David faced this when he went camping with a friend.

> I went camping with a friend and afterwards he rang me up
> and said, 'You know at the end of our camping weekend I
> wanted to give you a hug and I didn't.' And I thought, 'Wow!
> That would have been brilliant', and I'd actually thought the
> same, but we didn't.

Neither knew what the other would think so neither initiated it.

David's first thought after talking about this was, 'How often did my father cuddle me?'

Friendship is not a subject which can be talked about in a vacuum. It is a part of discussions about expressing emotion, masculinity and fatherhood, out of which men form views of both themselves and others. In many cases men viewed other men as conforming to a male stereotype and often distanced themselves from them. One of the problems with male friendship is that if two men both stereotype each other as being competitive, superficial and untrustworthy, then any friendship which does happen will be against the odds.

Some men didn't see friendship as being 'emotional'. Dennis found it difficult to express his emotions and didn't regard himself as an emotional person but friendships were important to him.

I find it difficult to express emotional relationships. We are good friends, we have plenty of banter and leg-pulling and things like this, but that is different, I think, than what you're looking for. And I don't think there's an emotional relationship there.

Andy saw relationships as primarily social and for Barney closeness did not have to involve intimacy. The men expressed very different ideas of what a close friend might be but a number defined 'closeness' in terms of trusting or confiding in somebody. Many also mentioned that they didn't know anybody they could trust enough to open up to them. It seems that men have to feel 'safe' in order to confide in somebody and often only find that degree of safety in their partner, a parent, or in somebody they have known for many years. The lack of trust of other men often meant that they were not prepared to become vulnerable themselves. For men, risk assessment is an important prerequisite to any friendship. As Brian and Martyn said,

There's very few men I would trust not to take the piss out of me if I overstepped a certain mark of self-exposure . . .

I would never let myself get into a position where I was beholden to another man, for any reason . . . I don't want to be at risk from another man.

Although men were diverse in their views on friendship they often seemed to be looking for something that they were convinced they couldn't have. Some of the men who did have strong relationships thought they had succeeded because the friends concerned had qualities which did not traditionally belong to men. Luke described his two close friends in the following way:

The thing that characterises both of them is that they are not manly men. They do not have a rigid view of themselves as men which precludes emotion or vulnerability. They are men who are willing to say they are not sure about things, they're willing to say they're frightened. They're willing to go against the male perceived things . . . Over the years I've had more women friends like that, who've been genuinely friends, than men.

Luke wasn't into 'men's pursuits like football' and found that when men are in a group they are boring because they are superficial. Friendship for him was more one-to-one. When the conversation turned to more personal issues, he thought that after a certain point men get frightened and don't want to talk about it. He had discovered that in social situations many men find it very hard to make conversation. They find it very difficult to talk to other people about themselves, but they love it if the other person talks to them about themselves. It's not a two-way thing. They don't talk about personal things because they fear that if they did, their identity would unravel and they would have nothing left.

I've actually found it more of a battle to make good male

friends than virtually anything else in relationships . . . To be honest with you, at a certain level I've given up on it, because as I've grown older I've just realised that what it needs for men to get close like that is for them to put some of the things about being men either on one side or to look at them more critically and there are very few men who are willing to do that.

Patrick felt that you had to be secure in who you were and what your interests were, especially if they diverged from the usual male interests. Being a man was

about really being very clear and honest about the things I like, the things I don't like, the things I will do and the things I won't do. And actually not feigning an interest or a concern in things that I don't like, even though they might be what men are supposed to do. So that, it's fine about the opera, the ballet, the reading novels, not knowing anything about how a car works; I haven't got a clue. I can put the petrol in, put the oil in, top up the windscreen wash, pump up a tyre and that's it. I'm in a motoring organisation for all that, and why not? And other men, if I say to them, I don't know how a car works, they'll have the bonnet of their car whipped open in no time and they'll be taking me through it in minute detail. It's like being with an anorak really, isn't it, it's awful.

Perhaps it is not surprising that some men had closer friendships with women than men. Richard's comment was typical of many:

I don't feel uncomfortable in the company of men but I just feel more comfortable in the company of women.

But in 'a world obsessed by sexuality', as Paul put it, many men thought that it was difficult to have close female friends without

110

inferring that it was a sexual relationship. For some men this was also a problem in the case of friendships with other men. David expressed the view that men backed off from close friendships because of their phobias about homosexuality, and Paul was of the opinion that single men who spent any time together were regarded as homosexual.

But in all-male settings this can sometimes be reversed. A chaplain in the Royal Marines writes the following,

> Deep friendships between men are a notable feature of service life. In Western culture, men, in contrast to women, are not noted for the closeness of their friendships. This may be because homophobia makes it difficult to develop emotional attachment without sexual feelings. The strong rejection of homosexual activity by the services, whatever else it may do, allows male-male friendships to develop: emotional attachments can grow freely as sexual feelings are directed to women, by definition outside the group.[1]

Or as Ronald puts it,

> I loved [Jim], stupid big cow, with my guts . . . Why did I have to come over here to this dirty butcher's shop of guns and broken bodies [WW1 trenches] to find it out. A man needs a woman but he needs a man too.[2]

With all this talk of men becoming more intimate, developing close friendships and showing their emotions, it should be remembered that men often relate well to one another by taking all the intimacy out of their relationship. Men can say things to one another which can appear to be very personal or even insulting but because the rules are understood they form a series of very effective connections with one another which depend on lack of intimacy and may provide the basis for humour. This can also take place in a meeting where both men and women are present, and it is very easy for women to misunderstand what is going on. For them these exchanges remain personal. So men must be careful that they are aware of their own way of operating. They need to discover intimacy and friendship, and they need to do it within a masculine context. It is not true that men need to abandon their ways of working and talking but they need to understand their own relational culture and women need to understand the way men operate. Perhaps the biggest single factor in this is the use of many different kinds of humour. In any group many types of humour are used to send signals from one man to another. From bonding, warnings, cynicism, exploitation, celebration, boundary crossing, shocking: a whole range of messages are conveyed not just by the words spoken but by a subterranean set of connections between men, from which most women are excluded. In other words the culture of man is still intact in ways which many men do not recognise for themselves. The desire to discover intimacy and expression has to be balanced against what can only be achieved in relationships by draining the intimacy out of them.

Many men look to women for intimacy because they expect a life-long relationship with a woman and love for that person to go together. In a society where that is the rule maybe it is valid and appropriate for male friendships to have a different emphasis. They can be based on companionship, shared interests, or activity without anybody thinking they are inadequate in some way. But that it is, in fact, not the current picture of the relationship between men and women. The high divorce rate and the high numbers of people living in single households lead us to draw two conclusions.

First, there is something wrong with the picture of deep and open intimacy between men and women within marriage. In many cases the needs of neither person are being met. In part this maybe due to the fact that our expectations of loving relationships have been built on fantasy rather than on reality. Our culture is not only obsessed with sexuality but with romantic fulfilment. From dating agencies, women's magazines and soap operas we are peddled the line that there is someone out there who is tailor-made for us. Our expectations are sky high and our disappointment at not finding the 'right person' correspondingly deep. Yet many successful long-term relationships begin by nurturing love rather than being bowled over by it.

Second, the need of every human being for love, acceptance and openness seems at face value to put men at a disadvantage. If their vision of lifelong commitment to a woman disintegrates, men may shut down emotionally. Alternatively, they may look for what they need in friendship with other men while at the same time being convinced that they will never find it. This is due to the fact that they believe the very stereotypes about other men which society perpetuates whilst rejecting them as being true of themselves. This is one of the important paradoxes about the difficulties in which men find themselves. If men do not know other men, or if in their friendships they stick to safe subjects, or to doing things together, then they may never test their assumption that at least some of the stereotypes are present in the men they are seeking to become closer to. However, many of them reject such stereotypes as being true of themselves. If both people in the friendship are doing this then they are in a tragic situation. The openness which could result in a close and appropriate friendship cannot exist while this catch-22 situation persists.

Men regard women as more fortunate in a world of broken relationships, as they can more easily find mutually supportive and open friendships with other women. If what I have described is the case then we would expect to see men increasingly under strain as they become isolated from human loving.

Drink and Friendship

For many of the men interviewed having a drink was very important. Going down the pub was an escape from domestic duties, a place of conversation and sometimes a place where friendship could be found. Steve spoke about drink enabling men to blurt things out that they had been bottling up. But drink can be destructive. Under its influence aggression could surface and relationships could be destroyed.

Keith is somebody who has a lot of male friends, many of them from a time when he lived in the south of England. He's lost contact with quite a few of them but feels that if he met them again he would be able to re-establish the relationships. Some of these friendships have been close. He doesn't do anything to maintain a friendship, but lets it run its course. He found out who his real friends were when he was down on his luck. For him men are attractive because of their sense of humour and personality. For many men, the big question is, 'can I get on with this person?' But what did Keith gain from his friendships?

> I get great enjoyment in being with them. When I used to go out drinking with them and going to parties and all that, I used to have a marvellous time in the evening. They were very good company. When you needed help as well, I got a lot of that from them as well, which really proved that they were genuine, really. This is when you find out, because I had great friends when I had a lot of money, spending it and saying, 'Come and have a drink'; you've got loads of friends then. They're all round you. Even I thought that they were friends. But then you find that when you're down in life, it's then you find out your friends. That's when I did find mine, anyhow, my genuine friends.

Keith had times when he was very happy and he enjoyed his emotions when he was like that. He was OK on recognising happiness. But he didn't recognise negative emotions until relatively recently.

Now I do, now. But then I didn't. Because I have never hit anybody in my life, but I have been extremely damaging verbally. I have been told this, afterwards. When I was having drinks and things, I mean. That I was completely acid verbally. Quite nasty, obviously, which I regret now, certainly. But I did know it a bit then, yes. It may be – chauvinistic might come into it – but I could knock a person down very quickly verbally, you see. I'd probably pick something wrong with them, which was quite nasty. That's not a nice way to be, I don't think, at all.

Keith was confused about why he had acted in this way. On the one hand he felt that this was his way of telling people the truth but it was also his way of competing with them and showing that he was mentally superior to them. Although he repeated that he had never hit anyone physically ('I don't think ever'), he did admit that he had been 'very, very nasty' especially when he was drunk.

Steve has several close friends.

My closest mate is somebody that I've known since I was at school and we can talk about absolutely anything, and we do. He might turn round and say, 'Sorry, I would never do that myself, but that's not the same as saying, 'You're a fool for doing it', it's just different ways of doing things.

[With others] you go out and you have a few drinks and you chat about what happened that week. That is a form of friendship, but it's not really deep, is it? Sometimes if things have built up, like you haven't got a clue where you're drifting on to, what kind of work you want to do or there might be various personal problems, something might have happened in the family, you've got to talk to someone. The more you talk, the more you realise that other people have had their own fair share of disappointment and sad events when they were young.

I might have two or three close mates that I would quite happily sit down and probably talk to them about anything, it wouldn't really matter. But out of the rest, you think, 'I think I'll just keep this to myself. This is bothering me, but . . .'

[There's a view that] if you've got problems you should always sort them out or talk them out with a woman, preferably your girlfriend, and everything will come out rosy. But that does tend to mean that you're in danger of having a lot of males going around that don't actually talk [to each other] about anything that's bothering them, which can't be very healthy, can it?

I mean, I've been in situations where I'm aware that some blokes – that I know through work or whatever – when they've had something to drink will just blurt out that there's some terrible calamity going on in their lives: one half of the couple is having an affair or something. They've bottled this stuff up and they release it and you think – I'm reliable enough to think I'm not going to go round saying, 'Hey, have you heard about this?' But it's a bit sad if you have to bottle it up to that sort of level. Clearly you want to talk to someone about it, but you don't feel able to.

. . . If there's a problem, men tend to clam up . . . to keep the pressure on. I think that's still true, though I think that is changing, or in fact I know it is because I have close relationships with my mates and we can talk about things, whereas I get the feeling that perhaps my father wasn't in that position. If he can't talk to me, perhaps that's because he couldn't talk to people at his own age, so I'm lucky in that respect.

Although drink can be a medium for conversation, several of the men in the interviews had been damaged by it or by fathers who became drunk. Overall, there was little evidence to suggest pubs were the ideal place to form close friendships. But the men seemed to have few other places where they could meet other men.

Yet again, women were seen as having a head start when it came to friendship. But the fact that women seem to be better at their kind of friendship does not mean that men have to be like them. Nor does it mean that because women are good at their form of intimacy and expression they are any more spiritual than men. Women also struggle with 'the darkness inside' which cuts them off from God and which calls them to renew their relationship with God. Perhaps what women *can* show men is how to work at relationships with others.

7

Listening to Other Men

One of the themes of this book is the importance of listening to men not only because this may help them but because men have a great deal to say which is helpful, wise, funny and enjoyable. Men are not second class citizens. When men listen to one another this can be a rewarding and even crucial experience because listening conveys love.

Theodore Zeldin, whom I have already quoted on the subject of conversation, has said:

> The ideals of conversation remained masculine until women changed the subject. They showed that talking about the emotions could not only improve the way the sexes treated each other but also diminish brutality and aggressiveness in general. This new conversation was like vegetarian cooking: it convinced only a minority. Most men continued to prefer the bawdiness, slapstick, shop talk or academic disputation which they could indulge in when women were not present.[1]

Of course, as we have seen, this is often true and men continue to find it difficult to talk and listen. But for those who do want to develop those skills the men's group is a possibility. In my previous book, *Men and Masculinity: From Power to Love* (London: Hodder & Stoughton, 1992), I talked about the early days of a group which had just started. It has now been going for nearly ten years. Over that time one person has left for a new job elsewhere and two others have joined. In terms of the life cycle of men we are all mid-lifers: 'Plateau Men'. The group is characterised by humour and friendship, and all the things and more that Zeldin says happen when men are on their own, but there is always space for someone to talk about an issue which is troubling them: illness, bereavement, family problems, stress at work, . . . whatever. Perhaps one of the reasons for this openness is that we have all come to the point where we needed to talk about some crisis and knew this was the place where people would actively listen to us without butting in with their own agenda. Help would be offered, or silence if that was more appropriate.

But perhaps what is most important is that the group is safe. There is a rule of confidentiality which means that although someone can repeat what they personally have said they cannot repeat what somebody else has said, even to their wife. This gives a great deal of security to those who make themselves vulnerable.

This group is not interested in some theoretical discussion of masculinity, in fact that is never discussed. It is a group of close friends who enjoy each other's company and who are there to listen when each of us faces the inevitable problems that come up. So this is not a group for a particular kind of man who is 'into' the issues. It is a possibility for anybody.

Some men will form groups which are active and do things together because they cannot bear sitting in a room chatting. Others will go for a pint every month but will make it a priority in their diary. It doesn't matter what the form is. All that matters is that men learn to listen to other men, support them and be supported by them. You don't even have to be emotional. You can start off with stony faces, hiding behind your masks. If you can keep it up for three meetings, shut the group down and watch the telly instead.

If we do want to change, and some of us don't, or to put it another way, if we do want to grow, then we have to take risks, and the risks of friendship can be considerable but rewarding.

The Possibility of Change

Men suffer if they can not let go of the mistakes of the past. This is why Christian spirituality is so liberating. It offers the possibility of forgiveness and with it the beginning of healing, especially the healing of memories.

When my children were very young, we used to read a book together about a girl frightened by a black cat. As she ran away from the cat it got bigger and bigger until it was larger than the houses. Exhausted, she stopped and faced the cat. The cat also stopped. She took a step forward and the cat stepped back. As it did so, it became smaller until they were back where they started, but the girl was no longer frightened.

Fear causes the dark to grow inside us. Things which others may feel are relatively unimportant can assume catastrophic proportions in our lives. This can lead to depression and worse, as we shall see.

Chris is somebody who feels unable to find a way of dealing with those things which he carries inside him. He finds relationships very claustrophobic. He feels under pressure to act in a certain way which is not the way he wants to act. He hates duty and responsibility. His frustration often ends in anger, which is the only emotion he feels he can show. At weekends he goes to the pub in order to get some space, but has had a bad time through drinking too much. He felt that conversations with other men were trivial and were not the places to discuss issues from one's own life. But he also felt that he was 'hopeless with women'.

Throughout the interview there were frequent recollections about his time at boarding school which he said 'took my spirit' and broke him. Some of the experiences he had there were too painful to talk about. He had never experienced a sense of freedom or had a childhood as he had taken on responsibilities within the family too early in life. ('I can't say that I have ever been happy'. Later he said, 'I wouldn't say I am a miserable person'.) All the available space inside him was filled with 'bad stuff' and it was those things from which he wanted freedom.

It's like a big lump of something really horrible, but you can't go and get it removed. Or you might be able to, I don't know; I've just never found a way of doing it. I suppose that this conversation has made me see that – I wouldn't actually have said that my life has been full of bad things.

Asked whether he believed that one could change as an adult he responded:

No. I think you can really, really want to; I think you can sit up late at night convincing yourself that tomorrow's going to be the start of a brand new day for you; a brand new person is going to emerge – and it never does because you've spent too long with the old one. Unless there was some way you could physically kill yourself inside, erase your memory and start again – because . . . I used to contemplate killing myself, just to see if I'd ever come back as something different.

Chris did not believe it was possible to reinvent yourself but if it was he thought it would be something a lot of people would be interested in:

I think if I could wipe my whole life off, or certain aspects of it, and fill them with better things, things I would have liked to have done if I hadn't been thinking about too many things, I'd do it. But you can't reinvent yourself. You can reinvent your looks and you can reinvent your personality to an extent – the way you speak to people, and you can change your accent and do this sort of stuff – there are external things you can change, but the internal things, the things that happen in your mind and your soul and stuff like that, not really, because you are a product of your environment and things that happen to you. If somebody could go inside and wipe them out and give you something nice, then I think quite a lot of people would do it.

The idea that Chris had considered killing himself was surprising because one of the things he was most afraid of was death. But as he commented himself, his answers weren't consistent throughout the interview.

. . . there are times when I am – I wouldn't say I'm happy; there are times when I'm relatively content, but there are times when I'm deeply discontented with life and the things that happen and those times can last quite a while, where I feel like I haven't done anything and I want to do something. That's probably where the death thing comes in and the fact that I'm so frightened of it, because I'm probably as frightened of death as I am of life. Because if I haven't coped with life, so if there's anything after death, what am I going to be like then?

But he loved his son and was able to tell him he loved him. Whether he would continue to be able to say it as his son grew older he didn't know. If he could give his son anything it would be optimism and a sense of self-confidence.

My dad has said it probably about three times to me. I know he does, but he's only ever said it about three times and they've been particularly emotionally charged times, otherwise, if we all went through hunky-dory, he wouldn't ever say it to me at all because we just know it's there and that's it, I suppose.

But at the end of the day, despite whatever's happened, I've got a chance to do something new. Maybe not for myself, but through my children anyway. So you never know.

I Don't Want to Talk About It

Of course as we have seen over and over again, men often don't want to talk about something which has gone wrong. Women will recognise this phrase as the answer men give when something upsetting has happened and their husband or partner shuts down and turns away. In the interviews some men said or inferred that 'I don't know whether to tell you this because I might get upset'. This was a phrase which occurred more than once as men struggled to talk about issues which were still raw. In this case it was Brian talking about the fact that he and his partner Christine could not have children. He felt that he had let his parents down who really wanted to have grandchildren, particularly his mother.

> I gave her an apron for Christmas once and she said, 'Oh that'll be a good one to bathe the grandchildren with.' Just slipping the knives in a nice velvet cover.

Not having children had made him think about life, particularly where his own life was going. With his brother and his wife not being able to have children either (for entirely different reasons) the family line was going to 'run out'. He felt that he was living in the past because there was nobody to hand things onto. Parenthood for him was about existing through your children. He hated his position. On holiday, when he and Christine were walking along a beach he got upset because he felt 'we ought to be doing this with some children'. The problem he has is the message he carries from his upbringing: 'Don't get angry'. He said: '. . . I very rarely get angry . . . I tend to turn things in on myself.'

Both men and women live with depression but it is only recently that thinking about male depression has begun to get through to people 'on the street corner'. Terence Real's best-selling book, *I Don't Want to Talk About It: Overcoming the Legacy of Male Depression*[2] tries to find a hopeful way out of depression for both overt and covert forms of depression which he maintains exist in men. He argues that many men have covert depression, hidden even from themselves, an unrecognised pain ticking inside them like a bomb waiting to go off. Men wait much longer than women before seeking medical help, they are less in touch with their bodies, but also conditioned to be more self-reliant than women. Those around them may not want to 'show them up' by raising the possibility that they may be depressed.

So the idea that women are more prone to depression means, in Real's opinion, that symptoms of depression in men may not be recognised as such. Problems at work, drinking, marital tensions may go undiagnosed. His claim is that overt depression in men is ignored while covert depression is hidden. If this is true then male depression sounds as if it is difficult to get at.

Real's thesis is complex and this is not the place to discuss it in detail. We know that there are many elements in depression including biochemical imbalances in the brain. Nevertheless, his case is interesting not least because in his conclusion he reflects the argument made in this book that men are in search of their soul. He talks about the achievement of masculinity not as a positive acquisition but as something negative, a disavowal. We have already seen how many men think of masculinity as a 'double negative' rather than as a positive. Men talk about not being a woman, not being weak or not being dependent.

As a result boys' acquisition of gender is a negative achievement. Their developing sense of their own masculinity is not, as in most forms of identity development, a steady movement towards something valued, so much as a repulsion from something devalued. Masculine identity development turns out to be not a process of development at all but rather a process of elimination, a successive unfolding of loss. Along with whatever genetic proclivities one may inherit, it is this loss that lays the foundation for depression later in men's lives.[3]

The trauma inherent in boys' lives can be grouped into three domains – diminished connection to the mother, diminished connection to aspects of the self, and diminished connection to others. Taken together these severances comprise what I call *the loss of the relational*.[4]

The boys who are happiest are not those with fathers who shut them off from those things considered feminine in the name of 'real masculinity', but those who nurture their sons. The happiest and most well adjusted boys are those with warm, loving fathers, fathers who have those qualities which are considered 'feminine'. The most important thing about a boy's relationship to his father is affection rather than 'masculinity'. If a boy is struggling psychologically it is likely to be because his father was abusive or neglectful. A nurturing father is a good father. But having a nurturing relationship with a son is also very good for the father. Such men have been shown to be 'healthier, less depressed and, surprisingly, more successful in their careers'.[5]

The problem is not with 'nurturing men' but with the kind of masculinity which calls this into question. It does so by perpetuating a distorted view of what it means to be a man which inevitably infers that if a man is a nurturer he is less not more of a man. Unless this view of masculinity can be challenged it will continue to perpetuate itself causing each generation of men and boys to suffer from the loss of the relational. Remember this means nothing less than a damaged soul: a withering of the 'person in community' at the heart of our humanity.

The most appropriate word to describe what needs to happen in men seems to me to be 'healing'. Men have taken a wrong turn, they are living with only half of their humanity[6] and that is distorted by the absence of the other half. In order to be healed men have to find a way to become fully human and to embrace the whole spectrum of human expression and being. Men have to find a way of turning back, of returning to the point at which the mistake was made and going back on the right road. But they need a role model they can look to who is himself living out what it means to be fully human and they will need support to become pilgrims (for pilgrimage it is) for the rest of their lives. This healing is not the stuff of a moment, a point of arrival, a glimpse of a new world, it is a direction for life. Men need to bring more to their families than their own inner resources. They need to bring a wisdom beyond themselves. They need (to use Real's term) to become a 'disciple' by finding a source of healing wisdom which can support those around them as well as leading them through life.

Several men in the interviews had suffered periods when they had been depressed. These periods sometimes lasted for as much as two years when they were unable to work. In some cases it was work itself which triggered the depression. Not enjoying a job, living with work stress or having bad relationships with colleagues were all mentioned. But the other area was the failure of relationships. Divorce or separation was in some cases so powerful in its impact that men became depressed for some time. This was made worse when legal battles lasted for a long time or when custody of the children was a real issue. It was also interesting that so many of the men talked about their lack of confidence, as if something in them was fragile and could be easily broken.

The Death of the Self

As long as there is something else to distract them such as a good job, an affair, or interesting leisure pursuits many men do not notice their isolation. It is when things go wrong that the world falls apart. Sometimes this results not only in depression but in suicide.

The suicide rates for young men are alarmingly high. They are the most vulnerable group in terms of suicide in this country.

In the UK 75 per cent of suicides are by men and suicide attempts by young men have doubled since 1985. The Samaritans themselves have attributed the rise to 'the pressure of modern day life combined with the traditional British stiff upper lip to form a cocktail of despair.[7] Simon Armson, Chief Executive of the Samaritans, puts the problem like this,

> The ability to listen to those in crisis can make the difference between life and death. Everyone has their own way of dealing with despairing friends. But the Samaritans' experience has taught us that some responses are more effective than others. Rather than distracting a friend from their sorrows with a joke, or by taking them to the pub, for example, helping them face up to problems by sharing their feelings tends to be more helpful in the long run.[8]

Stephen Fry, who is well known for his acting and writing has spoken in recent years about his own experience of despair. He is 'rich in family and friends' who would have helped when he was low but he didn't talk to them. Perhaps because he felt he would be diminished in their eyes or embarrassed:

> Of course we know that this isn't true and that our friends like us for our faults as much as our apparent virtues because we know that we can tell anything to our friends and family and they wouldn't judge us. But between knowing it and feeling it – the shame, the sense of embarrassment that we feel – is a huge gulf, between that and the knowledge that we ought to talk to anybody without them judging us. And it's that gulf that people throw themselves into when they become suicidal; the gulf between knowing that they ought to be able to talk to people and the knowledge that somehow inside they can't bring themselves to do it.[9]

Men seem to be particularly bad at bridge-building, between

knowing they should talk to somebody about their problems and doing it. Fry continues:

> We cannot bear the idea of talking about caring and feelings, and things, because we think it makes us look idiotic, particularly men of course. As we know this is the problem. Men just do not want to be seen talking about their feelings. They'd rather take their trousers down when drunk than take the shield off their heart for a second. We struggle about in the foothills of the emotions, wearing thorn-proof jackets, not very good at talking, and it seems to me that we must.[9]

It's easy to hide behind things, or status, or polite conversation. Or hide behind being one of the lads while hurting inside. Recently, a young man was drinking with his mates in the pub. After a few pints they went off for fish and chips and he said he would join them. He never did. The next morning he was found dead having committed suicide. No one knew why. His mother said, 'I wish I'd listened to him more.' The lads said, 'It's just not something you talk about with the lads. You don't want to appear soft.' We are all good at hiding what is inside us.

In the next chapter we move onto the subject of work. After several chapters on relationships it may look a bit out of place, but work has a unique place in men's lives. It is also one of the ways in which we express ourselves as 'soul' in that we are workers because God is a worker.

8

Working For a Living

Work gives us a sense of purpose and meaning. It is the means by which we both give and receive. It determines whom we associate with, where we live and how we see ourselves. What we do and how we do it affects how others see us and relate to us. But work is not just about what we do it is also about who we are. Ask a man who he is and he is likely to talk in terms of work. He is also likely to talk freely in a way he may not about other personal issues. It is his home territory.

Work is often the place where masculinities are shaped, challenged, and given meaning. Through work men give to the world, provide for those they love, seek advancement, carry responsibility and struggle with identity. Work is necessary to the soul; it is a blend of creativity and frustration in which we can either be diminished as human beings or become aware of the way in which recognition of its spiritual context can enable us to see what we are doing is contributing to a much bigger picture than we have ever been aware of before.

Think of the difference between good work and bad work. A job may provide us with money through which we can feed our families but little else. We have so much more to offer but instead of developing our gifts we find ourselves diminished. Our work eats away at us until we are either reduced to size or feel that we have to find a way out. Yet it is difficult to pin down any one job and call it 'bad work'. What one person finds debilitating another may enjoy. One man may find his fulfilment in leisure and family and may be quite happy with a job which is undemanding; another may throw himself into a job which consumes him but which he enjoys, even relishing the stress it brings into his life.

Throughout the world many people do not have the opportunities which we enjoy. Their lives are not protected by legislation or attention to human rights. There are those who are exploited, abused and who work in virtual slavery: child prostitutes, workers who labour for a pittance or who spend their lives in fear of those they work for. In our country we still have our sweat shops, and places of misery and fear where people work out of sight and out of mind. Yet for most of us the experience of work is a mixture of opportunity and frustration.

In a recent book entitled *God in Work*[1] Christian Schumacher puts forward the argument that work since the industrial revolution has become 'deformed' and that the growth of this kind of work is contributing to an unsustainable society. What is needed is a form of work which has 'wholeness' as its aim. For that to be achieved work must be organised around different principles. The dignity of the person, accountability of the firm, relationship to the environment, small units which emphasise relationship are all principles which are undermined by a deformed view of work.

Yet work can be very creative, offering chances to help others or to use our gifts. It can stretch us and offer us leadership responsibilities which we surprise ourselves in enjoying. Instead of putting our heads under the bedclothes on a Monday, we look forward to the challenge. We may leave one job, retrain and take on a new role, feeling that we now have a purpose where previously we had none. The world of work can be a world of possibilities.

For many work is the main focus of their spirituality. They may attend church and even find it encouraging and rewarding but know that on Monday they re-enter what they regard as the 'real' world. They spend most of their time working and share their lives with the community at work more than with any other group of people, including the family. They look for encouragement in the world of work not only personally but in the difficult choices they face there. It is by their work they are judged, respected and honoured or passed over and have to cope with failure. Those who have a Christian faith want the teaching and preaching of the Church to address them as workers not just people who have a religious faith. In other words the fact that spirituality is 'down to earth' is crucial here. Neglect work and you neglect the person.

Women have entered the labour force in unprecedented numbers in recent years and share many, if not more, of the pressures that men face. They are certainly as gifted as men in what they do and many men feel threatened by that while others welcome the end of injustice and enjoy working in partnership with women. Women frequently comment that the workplace is still a man's world. It is organised by men and for men and can be a foreign country to women.

One reason for this is that men have invested so much of themselves in work. For centuries this has been their world and it is not only a place of high reward but also high risk. Failure in the workplace breaks a man in two and threatens his whole world. Having given all to his job he can find that his investment in other parts of life is paltry. So many men are therefore driven to succeed because only by pushing harder can they avoiding sliding down the ladder into the unknown. This world is not necessarily organised around the children's timetable or the times of meals. It may not remember birthdays or special occasions. All kinds of things are hostage to the demands of work: even men's health.

In this arena women are being sold short. As we have seen in previous chapters the world of men has been kept together by a set of values which are distorted and which can cause people to disintegrate. In order to recover what has been lost while still supporting that world men have to recover a spirituality which can give them an alternative vision of life and culture based on the spiritual life. This does not mean that they necessarily change their jobs and become missionaries instead but it does mean that it is time for men to recognise that work can be destructive rather than creative. Women are entering that world, seeing it as a means of fulfilment and as the arena for expressing their gifts, at the very time when fundamental questions are being asked about how we work.

There is evidence that women are beginning to ask 'is it worth it?' because of the stress they are under. It is therefore equally important for women to prepare themselves spiritually for a working world which can destroy the soul. When women say that they are working in a man's world they are often talking about those destructive elements of work which a distorted masculinity has made possible or which lack of spirituality has made inevitable. The hope is that the insight of working women might be able to highlight dangers which are invisible to men.

Men on Work

How important is work to the men interviewed? Derek said,

> Well it is and it isn't. The sort of job I do, it's very easy to have tunnel vision and just become obsessed with it. A lot of people tend to have relationships outside work with people who they work with, so their life becomes very narrow and I don't want that at all. I'm married to someone outside work and when I leave work that's it: I don't discuss it at all. She's not interested, for one thing. And so that enables me to switch off. It is important in that I'd like to do well and I do my best, but I'm not as obsessed with work as some people who I see. I just see it as a means to an end, really, although I enjoy it when I do it.

Derek is aware of the insecurities of the job market and sees his friends, especially those from the old days, as providing a continuity and security which work cannot offer any more. As he looks forward to mid-life he feels a sense of anxiety.

> I do feel a bit insecure, I do worry about the future – not so much at this age, but when it comes to work it is a means to an end and you do need the money and today you see people thrown on the scrapheap at forty. There seems to be blatant ageism; once you're over forty, people don't want to know. If you were kicked out of one job, it would be very hard to get another . . . I try not to think about it too much, but I think it is a nagging fear that there is no such thing as a job for life any more and that some young, bright thing comes along in twenty years, they'll snap them up rather than you. That's one of the insecurities.

Bad Work?

Mark left school at 16 and went into a job which he 'hated from day six'. The job was so banal and repetitive that it got him down and made him feel that there was no point to it.

> I just thought they could make machines or train animals to do it, if animals would do that. They'd probably have more sense though.

After nearly three years of it he became quite ill as a result of it, getting very low and depressed on a Sunday night. He stuck it out because he didn't have any other options and family pressure was on him to stay. But he admitted,

> I took lots of time off work (my sick record was appalling). In the end they threatened to sack me.

He left before the end of his apprenticeship.

The headaches stopped as I walked down the steps and out of the building, having handed all my things back. It was amazing.

After a year on the dole he discovered nursing which he loved and which remains his profession.

But it is unfair to stereotype certain jobs as mundane. Steve was a clerk at a gas company and 'got a lot out of it'. It was his first job when he left school and it provided a foundation for learning about people and about himself. What is interesting is how much men talk about their work either in terms of what it does for them, or what place it had in their own pilgrimage, or what they felt they were able to do for other people though it. Somebody with a long work history may pick out those times when he was able to help somebody or when he felt he was contributing to something bigger. Of course this might be expected of people working as social workers, probation officers or teachers whose lives are full of opportunities to help others, but it is also true of men in other walks of life.

Tony who is now retired and in his mid-sixties had a very positive experience of leaving school at fifteen. For him work was one of the main contributors to his understanding of himself. In retrospect he found out that he did know what he wanted to do with his life even though he wasn't aware of it at the time. He wanted to be a chef and became an apprentice chef in his hometown. He stayed in the catering industry all his life, becoming a manager. His time in National Service matured him and enabled him to see that he was not destined to be a great chef which was why he moved into administration where he enjoyed a long and rewarding working life.

I consider myself to have been extremely fortunate to have spent a very happy working life and it has brought all sorts of material rewards which we might not otherwise have had. So we've been very, very lucky. Very lucky indeed in that respect

. . . If you don't enjoy your job that must be awful. That must be awful.

Michael was horrified when he was near retirement to discover that his life had been so dominated by work without him realising it.

In fact there was a time, some years ago, when everybody at work was encouraged to keep a diary of their activities throughout four consecutive weeks. I did this, I kept the diary as to what my activities were and I sort of grouped them into categories of home and family, work, hobbies, eating, sleeping etc. I found at that time I was working a 72-hour week, which made me realise just how busy I had been and just how little time I had had for the family. No. I was aware that I was very busy and didn't have much spare time, but I hadn't realised until I did that analysis that in fact it really did involve quite so much time, so that was quite a surprise to me.

I do have regrets about it. I think if I had my time again I would try to do rather less work than I've done and try and spend more time with the family. I now have grandchildren and I'm enjoying playing with the grandchildren enormously and being able to spend time with them. It would have been nice if I had been able to spend a similar amount of time with my own children.

Changing Role

It was a moot point whether Michael would be willing to go as far as Edward, who was doing just that. Edward had decided to stay at home and look after the children,

I was totally naive before I started, like any new mother. I don't really think there's any great difference between the sexes in that. I thought it should be easy to get the house painted and the garden done. But of course it's not like that at all; it's very demanding. I'm glad that I did it. Had I known how bad – how difficult – it was going to be, I would have stayed at work. I think at the time I felt that one of us should look after the children and in the event it proved to be me: one, on economic grounds; two because I'd been in the job for some years and I'd just drifted into it really. It wasn't my great vocation or anything. It was quite a pleasant working atmosphere; I could quite easily have just bundled along there for twenty years. This has given me a kick to get out and do something else, after I've brought up the children. Not that I really know what I want.

But how did people treat him as a man in that role?

I was, to an extent, one of the girls. I mean, people have been interested, I suppose. It's a topic of conversation . . . I think it's other people's perceptions, it's not mine. I think it's just no different. I suppose I'd always assumed, like most men, that women somehow know what to do. Of course they don't, just like I didn't. So I suppose that was an eye-opener, in that it certainly gave me a whole new respect for mothers, made me realise what women go through.

I don't feel that I'm belittling my sort of role, or betraying my role as the breadwinner . . . It's what I do; I'm very happy doing it. I don't miss anything really about work. Except conversation. Children aren't terribly good conversationalists about lots of – my vocabulary has shrunk as well. I find myself talking to someone, just cannot think of the word. But it's there, it just won't come out. So that's a bit of a downside to it.

A Fulfilling Job

It may be true to say that work is the focus of masculine identity but it is true in very diverse ways. In recent years discussion of masculinity (in the singular) has given way to an awareness that there are many kinds of masculinities. At work there are many different components to this. If the workplace is just composed of men then behaviour and attitudes will be different to situations where there are both men and women. Studies of miners show the strong sense of fraternity they develop which reflects danger, solidarity, community and equality. Their sense of identity is different from those working on the surface as management who have their own masculinities focusing on management, control, and authority. In his writing on men and work David Morgan also mentions the Newmarket 'racing lads' for whom the idea of 'bottle' is important.[2] It's an idea centred on nerve, control, and being able to 'take it'. Such men may see other forms of work as 'soft' because they do not exhibit the same themes as make up their own masculinity.

Other men live and work in contexts far removed from the world of danger and solidarity. In these circumstances it is evident that it is not enough to talk in terms of masculinity but it is vital to listen carefully to a personal story. Tradition will not help us in a situation where for instance a man has chosen an occupation which has continuity not with the tradition of the community but with lessons he has learned from struggles in his own childhood.

Dan's Story

Ask Dan what he looks forward to in his week and he will talk about his job working with children. Interacting with children is rewarding because they give so much but he also feels that he can give them something in return. It's a mutual relationship. Of course there are disappointments, especially with older children, but on occasion comments from them show that they are taking something in and that is rewarding. The children know that he likes being with them and is willing to sit and listen to them, and this is especially important for the teenagers. He finds children easy to work with because he doesn't have to prove himself, something he finds a pressure in other relationships. As a Christian Dan feels fulfilled when he becomes aware that God has used him in some way to influence them by passing on some wisdom.

When asked what this wisdom was and whether it related to insights he had learned in his own childhood, Dan said,

> I think being valued for who I was, by my parents in particular. It didn't matter what I achieved; there were no strings attached really. All they really wanted was for me to try my best and if I succeeded, fine, great, but if I didn't, never mind. I think that's something which a lot of people these days, and a lot of kids in this area, don't really have. There are so many pressures on children now at such an early age that this sense of achievement, I think, is a big one for many of them. They want to be accepted and not be different . . . the thing is to make them feel good about themselves – it's fine to be who you are.

He then told his own story which shows that who we are and how we face life affects how we work and the values we bring to it. In what follows it is worth remembering that Dan's work involves communicating, something he does not only with children, but also in his local church where he sometimes preaches.

As a child he had difficulty speaking and he had other educational problems. He was classed as 'slow'. Other children picked up on this and gave him a hard time. Eventually he went on to further education but he felt under pressure all the time.

I had to achieve to be accepted and I still carry that with me to some extent. I kind of feel that in order to be accepted, I can't be accepted for who I am; it's by what I do. That's quite a big issue sometimes, but I think it's getting easier.

I remember very vividly some instances when I was younger, five/six, coming in to a parents' party, or if they'd got friends round and chatting away to their friends and them just really turning round, patting me on the head, saying, 'Yes, very nice', and knowing full well they didn't understand. I hated it, so I used to just go and find my own quiet corner and just sit there. I used to hate it when my mum said, 'Come on, don't be shy, tell so-and-so . . .'.

Did his parents know how he felt? No. He didn't want to say anything because he didn't know how they would react. They may have felt that they had failed but in fact they were an enormous help to him and very loving.

With children he feels that he can be himself and does not have to prove himself but in some situations, including speaking at church, it is different sometimes. People see him as confident when he is not.

Perhaps I've learnt to hide it, which I did through my childhood. Again, I learnt to cope with different situations in the same way, by actually putting a mask on, if I can use that phrase, and not actually being me. Then I get frustrated at myself because, why? Why can't I just be me? Why do I feel I need to be someone which I think they want? . . . I think sometimes it's lack of confidence in myself, or being scared of being rejected, because of how I was as a child: because I didn't fit in so to some extent I was rejected by my peers. Perhaps I just don't want that to happen again.

Here is a man who enjoys his job and gets real pleasure from it. From his own account it would seem that the children he helps also enjoy what he has to say. He has a very clear philosophy and a message to pass on to them. It was not learned through his training or from books but from his own struggles as a child. Listen to him for a few minutes and the two halves of the story come together. His story demonstrates that we are whole people. We cannot separate who we are at work from who we are elsewhere although men frequently attempt to do this. We cannot separate who we were from who we are now.

Much of the pain experienced by the men interviewed has been to do with this issue. They have either tried to put the past into locked boxes or they have tried to be different people in different settings and have had a crisis of identity in mid-life as a result.

Listening to Men

Listening to men in the context of work may present entirely different opportunities to the ones we have seen so far. If it is true that men see work as a platform for personal identity, then this provides a very different way of meeting with them. The opening question people put to individuals on being introduced, asking them what they do, is frequently criticised as the wrong question. What we should do, we are told, is ask who they are. The latter is a question of relationship whereas the former is a question of function. But this is not so for men. There is a complex but significant interaction between what men do and who they are. Understanding the themes which come together to influence the masculinity of a particular workplace may give those prepared to listen some ideas about a man and his relationship to his work. Are we doing this to pry? No. We are doing this to love.

This is further underlined by the willingness of men to talk about what they do. Of course, it is a free world, and men are notorious for concealment and for wearing masks which prevent them being known. But in the case of many men active listening may mean that they are able to shift gear from description to engagement. Why should this be important? Perhaps because we need each other to help us discover who we are. We need feedback and also to be challenged as well as befriended. But primarily because work is only a part of the lives of men. It may be a dominant part but it is connected with the rest of the story of men's lives. If we listen both speaker and listener will learn.

Pretending to Have a Job

When Patrick gave up his teaching job he had a shock in store. He felt he had broken free and was delighted that he had been able to do it. All his life he had felt as if he was on tramlines set out for him by other people such as academic achievement, a secure job, social status and a reasonable salary. Although this was acceptable to his parents it wasn't to him. He also realised that he didn't like children very much! But when he found himself without a job he began to become aware how much his identity was bound up with his work.

> The other thing I look back on with some curiosity, is that I never told any of my neighbours that I hadn't got a job, so I would leave every day at the same time and go to the library or something, or arrange to meet my partner there and we would stay out. I would stay out the whole day.

Why did he do that?

> I think because − it's the shock bit. It's the bit about I'm supposed to be a professional, middle-class man who doesn't make decisions like suddenly giving up a job, and I've done that and that's not right. So I'm going to go on pretending to other people that actually that's what I still am . . . If I'd been

a bit more open and honest . . . I think that would have made life a bit easier than all this pretence and subterfuge and dishonesty.

Work is important to men, but it can become too important. Similarly the absence of work can be so devastating that men lose their sense of self-worth as well as their contact with the community. In a fast moving world where the pressure is on us we need to go against the flow and place our work in the context of a spiritual commitment which recognises the rhythm of work and rest, worship and function. But the good news from a Christian perspective is that all work contributes to God's purposes for the world. It is not only vicars and missionaries who are doing spiritual activities. Business men, train drivers and comedians are also involved.

Leadership

Most of those asked saw leadership as being about empowerment and building consensus. Richard, reflecting his own experiences of being a manager and being managed, spoke of a leader as 'somebody who empowers people to work within, or to extend, their capabilities'. For Patrick confidence and honesty were key qualities in leadership:

Good leadership, I think, is about first of all being confident about yourself and where you are and what you think and very clear about that and very willing to be honest about what you do well and what you don't do so well, and also to share that with other people and also to somehow bring about a climate of inclusiveness, so that everybody can feel part of the operation that's going on, the task that's going on and the goals that are to be achieved.

Mark spoke about having worked with some awful managers, but acknowledged that he was difficult to manage.

When we do group analysis or things, I always come out as a traitor or a cynic or a back-stabber or whatever it is. Not to people in the team, because I'll fall over myself to do things for them, but as far as managers go . . . and I'll do it to their faces as well. Lots of times you do hold back, but at certain times I've said things to managers and they've been very, very, surprised to hear, which has pleased [me] greatly. That's great. I don't see why you should hold back. There's no excuses for not doing it well, really, and there's shocking managers out there who haven't got a . . . clue and they ought to be told. I don't see that many people are told where they're going wrong, really. I'm not and it annoys me that nobody gives me constructive criticism. My manager at the moment, he doesn't say anything. I'd much rather know. I'd much rather know. But I've never really had a manager who's been particularly constructive in giving me balanced feedback, to tell me where I could improve.

Some men enjoyed being in a position of leadership. Luke enjoyed the power; Paul enjoyed the sense of control; Brian enjoyed the sense of achievement when it was possible to see others reaching their full potential; Barry enjoyed the sense of self-worth which it brought. Several mentioned that they liked getting positive feedback.

The pressures of leadership included worrying too much, almost a sense of panic, and the need to meet both your own and other people's expectations. For some, these pressures were not entirely negative. Barry commented,

[There will] be pressures but I hope those are healthy stresses that make me vibrant, push me to respond to challenges and move forward.

For others the pressures outweighed the pay-offs and several who felt they were cast in the role of leader outside their work were unhappy or ambivalent about it. John, Barney and Nathan were all unhappy about being seen as leaders, although despite his mixed feelings expressed below Nathan did finally conclude that he relished leadership.

I don't consider myself to be a leader and I don't push myself to be that sort of image of a leader. (John)

I actively try to go about not being a leader in things. I much prefer to let other people decide what they want to do and I'm usually quite happy to go along with that . . . it's not something that I feel particularly comfortable with. I would hate to think that people were basing their behaviour or beliefs or whatever on something I said. (Barney)

In the meeting . . . I got pushed forward as the person who was going to front this evening and I remember thinking, 'Oh God, not again.' I felt like I was the only person who was doing anything . . . Anyway, we had the meeting and I suddenly switched into Mr Personality . . . I was having to move it along all the time and I just did that in a way which made the evening fun . . . It came across well and I know it did because people said it did. At the same time I'm thinking, 'I don't want to be doing this.' (Nathan)

Only one man had a different approach and that was Frank who focused on the need for a leader to have confidence to lead from out front.

I think they [leaders] have to have a deep belief in themselves and their own capability. To make decisions about what's right and wrong, that's a personal decision and a good leader's a person who can see that through and come out having made the right decision . . . leadership is about not necessarily doing it by the will of the majority; the confidence to do it and take

others along with you, not necessarily by agreement but by
leadership.

9

The Whole Man

Now we have heard what the men interviewed have had to say about their lives. They have talked about their experience of those key areas of life which together make up the foundations of the spiritual: our personal identity, our relationship with God, our relationship with others and our relationship with the world through work.

In many cases they were sceptical about the whole idea of the relevance of spirituality to their lives. But interestingly it did seem to be something which was important even to those who did not have a formal commitment to religion. The aim of spirituality is to become a whole person not only in a personal sense but in terms of our relationships and in our relationship to the world primarily through our work. In every aspect of men's lives examined here there is promise and celebration, but there is also an enormous amount of pain.

Again and again we have seen that one of the main ways in which men can grow to wholeness is through listening and being listened to. Listening conveys love: even if only for a few moments, it counts the other person as more important than ourselves. In every area of life that we have covered men need to open up the possibility of listening. Workers need to be listened to in order to participate in work and to feel they have dignity. Otherwise they may feel that 'monkeys could do the job better'. Men need to listen to one another, to fathers and mothers, to the women in their lives. But how do men learn to listen? It is here that the spiritual agenda becomes vital. In recovering the spiritual life, in recovering our soul, we renew a relationship which we have struggled to live without. In the relationship with God we meet with unconditional love and discover the ability to trust someone with our lives. In confession and contemplation we hear our own voice and learn from that. In waiting, in silence and in becoming immersed in the Scriptures we grow spiritually. If we are fortunate as a society we will rediscover these truths again.

Pilgrims without a Destination?

There is a world of difference between living with uncertainty and living by faith in a world of uncertainty. Life has always been uncertain and much harder in previous centuries than it is now. Anybody looking at the sophisticated society we have built for ourselves might believe that we have 'sorted it'. However, in terms of human relationships the true picture is quite the opposite. We are not only a consumer culture, we are also a therapy culture, a divorce culture, a broken family culture, a culture of abuse, a racist culture. In short, we are letting each other down and mistrust is growing, which is fatal to any community.

Clifford Longley recently put his finger on our condition when he said, 'Western civilisation suffers from a strong sense of moral and spiritual exhaustion. Having constructed a society of unprecedented sophistication, convenience and prosperity, nobody can remember what it was supposed to be for.' The uncertainties and insecurities of our lives are changing the way we live. Having done away with God there is nowhere to go.

Oxford philosopher Zygmunt Bauman draws two pictures of the plight of men and women in our society. One is the *vagabond*, the other is the *tourist*.[1] The vagabond moves from place to place, not sure about where he is going next, always moving on, never stopping for long.

What keeps him on the move is disillusionment with the place of the last sojourn and the forever smouldering hope that the next place that he has not visited yet, perhaps the place after the next, may be free from faults which repulsed him in the places he has already tasted. Pulled forward by hope untested, pushed from behind by hope frustrated . . . The vagabond is a pilgrim without a destination; a nomad without an itinerary.[2]

Or if you prefer you could choose the picture of the tourist. Again the tourist is a person with momentum, moving on all the time. Whatever the history of places visited, for the tourist their only significance is their appearance in his own biography.

The tourists pay for their freedom; the right to disregard native concerns and feeling, the right to spin their own web of meanings, they obtain in a commercial transaction. Freedom comes in a contractual deal, the volume of freedom depends solely upon the ability to pay, and once purchased, it has become a right which the tourist can loudly demand, pursue through the course of the land and hope to be gratified and protected . . . physically close, spiritually remote: this is the formula of both the vagabond's and tourist's life.[3]

There is no sombre burdensome moral responsibility in either life. They are packaged away, whisked away. With no responsibility for the evils of the places they visit, the tourist is bad news for morality. They 'pass through'.

Perhaps men are on the move from being the rational, controlling decision makers that they were to admitting, in the midst of the crisis of masculinity, that they are lost in a far more fundamental sense. They are nomads who are 'pulled forward by hope untested, pushed from behind by hope frustrated'. Here then are the two faces of the self: the rational, controlling decision maker and the vagabond or tourist. The former is recognisable as the face of men in the modern world. But recently things have changed. Religion, for example, has become an alternative leisure pursuit. Some people play golf on Sunday, others go to church. We are all 'just passing through' and, as long as we can agree that we are not going anywhere and are not accountable, then it's pretty much up to the individual what he does.

These may be the two faces of the self but neither are windows on the soul. Whereas the vagabond is a pilgrim without a destination, the essential mark of the pilgrim is that he has a destination. In Christian thought and practice that destination is guaranteed by the resurrection of Jesus Christ from the dead. If Christ is dead there is no destination, no point in thinking about spirituality. The whole foundation of Christianity is based on that one historical act of Christ defeating death. So Christian spirituality is a pilgrimage towards a goal guaranteed by the resurrection and that is why Christian hope is not tentative but a celebration.

Notes

1: What is Man?

1. Sam Keen, *Fire in the Belly* (Bantam Books, 1991), p.6.
2. Robert Hicks, *The Masculine Journey* (Navpress, 1993), p. 132.
3. Jack Balswick, *The Inexpressive Male* (Toronto: Lexington, 1998), p. 97.
4. J. Pleck, *The Myth of Masculinity* (Cambridge: MIT Press, 1982), p. 147, quoted in Balswick, p. 97.
5. See chapter 8 on work.

2: Glimpsing a New World

1. Zygmunt Bauman, *Legislators and Interpreters* (Cambridge: Polity, 1989), p. 189.
2. In his Wilberforce Lecture, 1998.
3. Theodore Zeldin, *Conversation* (London: Harvill Press, 1998), p. 3.
4. Petitioning means asking God for something.
5. Malcolm Allison, 'Sayings of the Week' in *The Observer*, 14 March 1973.
6. Nick Hornby, *Fever Pitch* (London: Gollancz, 1992), p. 72.

3: Why Bother with Religion?

1. Sam Keen, *Hymns to an Unknown God:Awakening the Spiritual in Everyday Life* (London: Piatkus, 1994), pp. 76–7.
2. In 'Genetics', an interview with Prof. Steve Jones, in *Third Way*, February 1999, 18.
3. Mark Greene, 'One in two preachers aren't relevant' in *Quadrant*, November 1998.
4. Peter Brierley (ed.), *UK Christian Handbook: Religious Trends 1998/9* (London: Christian Research), No. 1, table 5:13.
5. Peter Brierley, *Christian England* (London: MARC, 1991), p. 79.
6. Grace Davie, *Religion in Britain since 1945: Believing without Belonging* (Oxford: Blackwell, 1994).
7. Taken from E. Jacobs and R. Worcester, *We British: Britain Under the Microscope* (London: Weidenfield and Nicholson, 1990), cited in Tony Walter and Grace Davie, 'The religiosity of women in the modern West', *British Journal of Sociology* 49, issue 4.
8. Walter and Davie, 'The religiosity of women in the modern West', 640–60.
9. ibid., 119–20.
10. ibid.
11. Galatians 5:22.
12. Jürgen Moltmann, 'Unfinished Business' in *Third Way*, vol. 49, no. 10, pp. 12–16.

4: Fathers and Sons

1. Nelson Mandela, *Long Walk to Freedom* (London: Abacus, 1994), pp. 32–3.
2. The story of the son who left home in Luke 15:11–32 contains a powerful image of unconditional love.
3. Terence Real, *I Don't Want to Talk about It: Overcoming*

the Legacy of Male Depression (New York: Fireside, 1997), p. 143.

6: Men and Friendship

1. 'Towards a Christian Masculinity for the Armed Forces', unpublished thesis, unattributed.
2. Cited in John Smith, 'Men must learn how to love', *Third Way*, December 1995.

7: Listening to Other Men

1. Theodore Zeldin, *Conversation* (London: Harvill Press, 1998), p. 12.
2. Terence Real, *I Don't Want to Talk about it: Overcoming the Legacy of Male Depression* (New York: Fireside, 1998).
3. ibid., p. 130.
4. ibid., p. 137.
5. ibid., p. 323.
6. ibid., pp. 226–7.
7. Report on Suicide from the Samaritans, 2 November 1992. The quotation is from Simon Armson, then Chief Executive of the Samaritans.
8. From *Listen Up: Responding to People in Crisis*, www.Samaritans.org.uk/ListenUp
9. www.samaritans.org.uk/sams.html/fry.html

8: Working for a Living

1. Christian Schumacher, *God in Work* (Oxford: Lion, 1998).
2. David Morgan, Discovering Men (London: Routledge, 1992), p. 77.

9: The Whole Man

1. Zygmunt Bauman, Post-modern Ethics (Blackwell, 1993).
2. ibid., p. 240.
3. ibid., p. 241.

Appendix

These are not biographies but a collection of facts, summaries and quotations which may help to jog the reader's memory about who is who. There is no particular order to the elements included – they are solely there as an aid to memory. They are compiled from the interviewee's own words but their selection is of course subjective. Every attempt has been made to preserve the anonymity of the interviewees. In some cases, details have been omitted or replaced with broad references to 'social' or 'education' sector or other equivalents. Nottinghamshire can be a very small place! If a name which is listed here does not appear in the book, this may be because others have covered the same points, or because the interview has been used as background material. The information included here refers to the period when the interview was conducted, not to the current circumstances of the men involved. The phrase 'middle-aged' is used 'loosely' as there does not seem to be a scientific way of measuring it!

Ahmed Young, single, no children. Comes from a close Moslem family. Likes to have time on his own. Has travelled widely. Musician. 'I like to be in control of my own environment.' 'I'm quite happy with my life.' 'I'm not religious at all.' 'Spirituality is important to me – its about the essence of the person.'

Andy Describes himself as working-class. Step-father to two boys raised from infancy. 'I love my wife a lot, I think the world of her.' Had a happy childhood but also got into trouble with the police. Not in good health. Recently converted to Christianity.

Barney Young, married, one daughter. Had been in a serious road accident. Unhappy at work, and wants to open a small business instead. 'Stubborn.' Catholic background. 'Spirituality is a belief in some other dimension of our lives.' 'Being non-judgemental is important in friendships.'

Barry Middle-aged, divorced and remarried with two children. Works in social sector. In conflict with his first wife over custody of their two children – he has custody. Very stressed. Proud of being a father. 'Football is an escape.' 'I'm passionate about life.' 'I hesitate to say I don't believe in God just in case.'

Ben Middle-aged, married with children. Works in education. Enjoys job very much. 'I'm not a particularly deep person.' Keen football supporter. 'I don't think you need to be religious to be a spiritual person.' 'What motivates me is wanting to change.' 'I don't often get unhappy.'

Brian Middle-aged, living with partner. Football very important. Under-confident but 'the same person all the way through'. He and his wife cannot have children. Doesn't trust men. Avoids anger, cries a lot. 'No massive highs, no massive lows.' Indecisive. 'I'm not a practising Christian now.'

Charles Near retirement, married twice. Works with people. Applied for ordination but was told he was too old. Started going to church in adulthood having not gone since his youth. His mother had just died. Feels strongly about inequality and violence. 'I've really been extraordinarily fortunate.'

Chris About 30, married with children. Needs space and finds relationships restrictive. Burdened with too much responsibility as a child. Likes rugby and the pub. Believes in personal dignity not God. 'Boarding school took my spirit.' 'If I had my choice I would never have lived.' Only emotion he expresses is anger.

Dan Young, engaged. Works in education. Had speech problems as a child. Felt if people really knew him they would reject him. Christian who feels that prayer and studying the Bible are essentials. 'God does care.' Has had close friends but no male friends at the moment.

David Middle-aged, married, three children. 'I have a big thing about being a good dad.' Lacked self-confidence as a child. He is a leader at work which is stressful but fulfilling. Relaxes by gardening. 'I'm aware now of the lack of a good male friend.' Brought up as a Christian but is rethinking his faith.

Dennis Retired, married with two adult children. Disappointed when children stopped attending church. Very straight with people. Competitive. Loves fishing. Has a number of friends who go back a long way. Finds it difficult to express emotions. Christian 'but doesn't understand it'. Practical person.

Derek Young, married. Works in media. Concerned about future job security. Deeply affected by his mother's mental illness some years ago. 'Life is about relationships not money.' 'You can love your job but it won't love you back.' 'When we die we die.' 'I do believe in the force for good.'

Edward Married, middle-aged, seen as extrovert by others but really quite shy. 'Bland – no hidden depths.' Wife works full-time and he has full-time care of his daughters. Younger brother died in his teens. 'You don't have to be spiritual to lead a moral life.' Has a sense of awe in old churches, but is not a Christian.

Errol About 30, married with children. Busy church life. Prayer is really important. Works in business in an all-male environment. Birth of first child was a very emotional occasion. Deep respect for other religions. Picky about male friends because of one-upmanship. Passionate about racial injustice. Patient.

Frank In late middle-age, two adult children. Studying for a new career. Remarried soon after his first wife died. Worked in business. Facing financial hardship and is very stressed. Very busy church life but feels a sense of achievement. Thrives on leadership. 'Tolerance is not something I am known for.'

Gordon Middle-aged, divorced, has children. Now living with gay partner. Works in social sector. Likes clubbing – 'even at my age'. Thinks people hide behind roles – 'I lived in denial'. 'Everybody is a spiritual person.' Sees religion as oppressive. Loves the beauty of the countryside. 'I do need silent times.'

Jerry Young, living with partner, self-employed in construction. Blunt. 'Working-class background.' Two close male friends. Father was an alcoholic but hardworking. Loves travelling: 'It's a buzz – I've tried drugs'. 'The universe is too vast not to believe in something.' Scared about the future. Loves music.

Jim Young, single, ambitious. Outgoing but 'loves personal space for thinking'. Being accepted is essential. Friends are important but only has one close male friend. Cries easily. Ending a long-term relationship was devastating. Very distressed by the death of his grandfather.

John Middle-aged, married with children. Job-seeker, doing a counselling course. 'A caring person.' Christian who returned to church life in his thirties. He and his wife had a stillborn child. His coping strategy is 'letting go'. A business venture had recently failed. 'I try to be the same person with everybody.'

Josh Middle-aged with two children. Christian. Considered missionary work when younger. 'Seen by others as arrogant' but sees himself as insecure. Not motivated by materialism. Still talks to his father though he's been dead for decades. Thinks people can change and take the masks off. 'Happy.'

Keith Middle-aged, single. Was a manager in a large company. Now does voluntary work with disabled people. 'I absolutely love them.' Had a bad time with alcohol earlier in his life. 'For a few years I had no purpose.' Bullied at school by a teacher. Felt let down by Christians when he needed them. Shy.

Larry Middle-aged, married with children. Works in public services. A Christian with many responsibilities at church. Became a Christian as a teenager. 'Prayer has become really important.' 'I repressed my feelings until a few years ago.' 'Now I see myself as a father.' 'I'm not a self-motivating person.'

Len Middle-aged, separated, with teenage children. 'Gutted' by his wife leaving home. Enjoys job in education. Had a period when overwork lead to depression. Relaxes by gardening. Musician. Christian. Enthusiastic about church life. Thinks it's easy for men to form close friendships. Happy childhood. Untidy.

Luke Middle-aged, living with partner. 'Good at job.' Loves walking and swimming. 'Talks too much.' Tough teenage years when he lived on his own. Gets a great deal of pleasure from his children. Works with children and families. Wants peace and space for reflection. Was a Christian but is not now.

Mark About 30, living with partner. Left school at 16 and had a bad time on drugs and drink. Job was routine and boring. Retrained and changed to working with people. Had a difficult time with a girlfriend who had mental health problems. Good leader but poor at the 'human stuff'. Thinks religion has no meaning. Honest.

Martyn Middle-aged, divorced with two children, living with partner. Feels discriminated against because he is a man. Distrusts men. Nursed his wife after an accident: she then left him. Believes Christ, Buddha, Mohammed were all sons of God. 'Women have something more, women have the power of life.'

Matt Middle-aged, married, works in education. Christian, and involved in church life. 'Jesus is real.' Very musical. Only talks openly to his wife but has male friends. Considers being honest, loving, humble and confidential to be important. Can have a short fuse. Thinks that to be masculine is to be in control.

Michael Elderly, married with adult children. Retired from the educational sector. Has no close male friends, which he sees as 'unfortunate'. Enjoys painting. Over-commitments at work led to limited time with his family, which he now regrets. Bottles up emotions. 'I do count myself as a Christian.'

Nathan Young, married, works in financial sector. Articulate. Hates violence – especially war. Outwardly confident but has a fear of failure. Approachable. TV addict. Very involved in church life. Bought up in Catholic family. Doesn't rate male friendships but has one good friend. Sees crying as a loss of control.

Nick Middle-aged, married with children. Self-employed in construction. Does voluntary work with children. Became a Christian after his wife was healed. One of his biggest problems is not having any close friends. 'Men will not let go and give themselves.' Finds it easier to get on with children than adults.

Oliver About 30, married, working in education. Christian with strict upbringing. Addicted to music. Football is important to him. Finds it difficult to express emotion. Feels rootless. 'I'm always inquisitive, I always want to learn new things.' 'Going up in the mountains, that was really profound.' 'I'm still cynical.'

Patrick Middle-aged, living with partner, with teenage children. 'We do a lot of things together.' Works in social sector. Enjoys job but can't wait to retire. Likes choral music. 'I hate football.' Would become a Catholic but unfortunately is an atheist. 'I don't even pray for Labour to win elections.' Can be sulky.

Paul Middle-aged, single. Christian. Finds it difficult to talk about feelings. Does a lot of voluntary work with young people. Involved in leadership in the church. Studying for degree. 'You can't change the world but you can change your bit.' 'If you don't take control of your life, others will be in control of it.'

Richard Middle-aged, divorced and living with a partner. Has two children. Doesn't enjoy his work. Has only ever had one close male friend who has now moved away. Thinks of himself as a lazy person but also as a leader. Had a very hard time when unemployed. Passionate about football. 'Not religious.'

Simon About 30, married with children. Works in the business sector. Finds being a father fulfilling. Quiet on the surface, stubborn underneath. Father died when he was young. Has Christian companions. His wife is his best friend. Underwent a Christian conversion when a young adult. Prayer is important to him as is Christian fellowship. Passionate about football.

Steve About 30, single, recent graduate. Job-seeker. His brother died when he was very young which he 'never really dealt with'. He has a close male friend. 'We can talk about absolutely anything.' Would like his obituary to read, 'He was a bit of a laugh but sometimes he drank too much.' 'I'm not religious.'

Timothy Middle-aged, living with partner. No children. Politically active. Catholic upbringing. 'Concerned about the world.' Inclination to laziness. Sees himself as a humanist. Footballer. Loves exotic holidays. Thinks that spirituality is about 'feeling your life has been given to you and you've got to do something useful with it'.

Tony Retired, married with two adult children. Catering background. Very involved in voluntary sector. Happy childhood in large family. 'I tend to be a fairly objective person.' Influenced by visiting the third world. Active churchgoer. 'You express the fact that you're a Christian by the way you conduct yourself.'